Open-Hearted Ministry

P9-CLO-333

'FROM BEITA GILL-AUSTERN

Prisms

The Prisms series explores issues pertinent to renewing congregational life and clergy identity in an era of deep confusion and rapid change.

Open-Hearted Ministry

Play as Key to Pastoral Leadership

Michael S. Koppel

Fortress Press
Minneapolis

OPEN-HEARTED MINISTRY
Play as Key to Pastoral Leadership

Copyright © 2008 Fortress Press, an imprint of Augsburg
Fortress. All rights reserved. Except for brief quotations in
critical articles or reviews, no part of this book may be
reproduced in any manner without prior written permission
from the publisher. Visit http://www.augsburgfortress.org/
copyrights/contact.asp or write to Permissions, Augsburg
Fortress, Box 1209, Minneapolis, MN 55440.

Scripture quotations are from the New Revised Standard
Version Bible, copyright © 1989 by the Division of Christian
Education of the National Council of the Churches of Christ in
the U.S.A. Used by permission. All rights reserved.

Cover design: John Goodman. Cover images: (from top to
bottom) © iStockphoto.com/John Hawthorne;
© iStockphoto.com/Jeremy Voisey; © iStockphoto.com/Roberta
Casaliggi. Author photo courtesy of Shan Mohammed.
Interior design: Allan S. Johnson, Phoenix Type, Inc.

Library of Congress Cataloging-in-Publication Data

Koppel, Michael, 1963–
    Open-hearted ministry : play as key to pastoral leadership /
Michael Koppel.
        p.   cm.
    Includes bibliographical references and index.
    ISBN-13: 978-0-8006-6295-0 (alk. paper)
    1. Pastoral theology.   2. Play — Religious aspects —
Christianity.   I. Title.
    BV4011.3.K67   2008
    253 — dc22   2008010049
    ISBN 978-0-8006-6295-0

The paper used in this publication meets the minimum
requirements of American National Standard for Information
Sciences — Permanence of Paper for Printed Library Materials,
ANSI Z329.48-1984.

Manufactured in the U.S.A.

12   11   10   09   08   1   2   3   4   5   6   7   8   9   10

Contents

Preface

The enthusiasm of our call to ministry generates enormous energy, yet over time something happens that slowly drains this energy from our lives. We feel as if we have been robbed. Sometimes it happens rather abruptly, as if an intruder has entered the house of our own souls and demanded something precious from us. We give in, however reluctantly; the robbery takes an emotional toll. What once was lively and energetic inside of us suddenly feels empty.

Sometimes the process is much more subtle — not overtly intrusive, but insidious nonetheless. The intruder steals a few things when we aren't home. The changes are not really noticed. In time we gradually wake up to the reality that something has happened. We may choose to go in search of the robber and the missing items. We also may just ignore it or even deny that anything has happened.

An image of theft is, of course, one that depicts how it feels to have the joy of life taken from us. Whether the loss occurs suddenly or gradually, we realize that we have been robbed of our enthusiasm for ministry. Whether we have given ourselves over too readily to the expectations of the community or institutional church or have locked ourselves in so tightly to our own expectations of ministry, we are left feeling depleted, ineffective, and grim. We are unsure of the way forward, yet doing nothing is perilous. We hesitate, having lost that which we wanted to give.

The church needs leaders who can tap the vitality of God's call that originally brought them to ministry. Such energy is fresh, responsive, and contagious. Pastoral leadership involves experiencing, and making possible for others to experience, the joy of life and faith. This book proposes that through play we can connect with the source of this passion. Yet we often focus our energy in areas that do not serve this end. We become depleted in any of a number of ways:

- chasing institutional demands,
- meeting expectations or pleasing people in the congregation,
- guarding against mistakes that lead to criticism,
- performing too many thankless tasks, and
- spreading ourselves too thin with "yes" too often and "no" too seldom.

Continually conforming to the expectations of others sets us up for failure and stifles our God-given energy.

Early in ministry I had what I call my airplane dream series, a collection of dream images that prompted me to embrace my internal misfit. I dreamed of an airplane traveling down a country road and stopping at a red light. In another of my dreams, a plane is trying to maneuver through a parking garage meant for automobiles. Clearly, planes don't fit in garages and they certainly don't belong on country roads. An airplane in those places simply doesn't "fit." Similarly, my passion for ministry was restricted by the environment. My dreams indicated the need for a transition to a new context, one that would nurture my internal misfit. In the intervening years, I have learned that claiming my misfit nature allows for the expression of exuberance, flexibility, and humor rather than anger and frustration.

Pastoral leadership can benefit from a playful attitude and posture that bridges the gap between deadness and life, between listlessness and vitality. We navigate this tension in ministry not by ignoring the energy depleting aspects, but by working with — dare I say playing through — them with renewed perspective and vigor. *Play* is the term I use to describe this *pattern* of relationship with others and *perspective* of viewing ministry. My definition of play has evolved through years of ministerial practices in various contexts: *play is structuring chaos*. A playful perspective and pattern takes to heart the necessity to engage creatively within changing contexts of ministry. Play as structuring chaos means that pastoral leaders must relate within structure, and guide others to do so as well: structure means ethical standards direct the behavior of ministers and church members as well as the practices of Christian communities. Chaos names the way in which we often experience the unknown, the unpredictable, and the novel. Pastoral leadership as artful and creative play navigates between known and unknown, predictable and unpredictable to embrace the living God of Creation at the center of purposeful and faithful ministry.

This book does not provide a blueprint of how to engage in each and every task of ministry, although it will make practical suggestions along the way. Nor does it suggest that one size or type of ministry fits all. Instead, it offers the realization that discerning your path in ministry requires development of your own inherently good gifts. This book invites you to claim or reclaim your passion, so that you may connect with the restorative, healing, and empowering energy necessary for ministry.

This book may benefit newcomers to ministry as well as those ripened with experience. Those with energy will be prompted to own personal strengths and develop practices to sustain that energy. Those who have lost touch with the original passion for ministry will find ways to reconnect with sources of vitality. For everyone, this book offers a fresh perspective and valuable practices that will transform you and your effectiveness in ministry.

This book is based on a course I've taught for several years, which has confronted a fair share of skeptics.

An experienced pastor working toward an advanced ministerial degree could not conceive of any benefit from a course in creativity and play theory. This pastor typifies the suspicion that some ministerial leaders harbor. To his mind, ministry and the academic study that undergirds it require seriousness. He wondered whether anyone in his judicatory or congregation could take him seriously if he was engaged in the study and practice of play. He enrolled in the course reluctantly at the program director's recommendation. Through study and enactment of play in the course, and with critical reflection on ministry in his small, rural, southern congregation, this pastoral leader eventually realized that a theology of creative play has helped him and his congregation imagine new possibilities for ministry and celebrate the journey thus far. The pastor now sees play and creativity at the heart of the gospel.

So I extend an invitation to you: let this book become an exercise in creative play. My hope is that when you have finished reading, you will have played with new ideas and practices for ministry.

Acknowledgments

Many have accompanied me on this creative and playful journey of research. My heart is full with gratitude as I recall the great company of people, those named and the many left unnamed, who have enlivened this effort.

I give thanks for the opportunity to teach on the faculty at Wesley Theological Seminary in Washington, D.C., where students in all of the degree programs continually spark my imagination; for the vision and leadership of President David McAllister-Wilson and Dean Bruce Birch; for faculty colleagues, especially Denise Dombkowski Hopkins, who has guided me through this project with compassionate care, and Mary Clark Moschella, Sharon Ringe, Beverly Mitchell, and Larry Stookey who have provided emotional and intellectual sustenance; and for those who read early drafts of this writing, namely Lew Parks, Lovett Weems, and Fredericka Berger. Staff colleagues Rebecca Scheirer and Sara Sheppard have provided helpful editing and technical support.

Mentors at the Claremont School of Theology, Kathleen Greider and Bill Clements, influenced the topic choice and indelibly formed my identity as a pastoral theologian and caregiver. Colleagues in the Society for Pastoral Theology have thoughtfully engaged this work. Thanks to Charles Scalise and Roslyn Karaban for an opportunity to present material in the Church and Christian Formation study group; and to Kristen Leslie for helping me to make the connections. My appreciation extends to the editorial team at Fortress Press, notably Michael West and Carolyn Banks. A sabbatical research leave from Wesley Seminary and a Summer Research Fellowship from the Wabash

Center for Teaching Theology and Religion provided time for reflection and writing.

Friends and family have nurtured my spirit through the years. For Eva Lew, Marjorie Purnine, Kevin North, Russell Scott, David O'Malley, and for Melissa, David, and Dylan Kirk, I remain ever thankful. I celebrate and honor the congregation of my childhood, St. Stephens Presbyterian Church, in North Highlands, California, for nurturing creative faith. I dedicate this book to my parents, Adalbert S. and Sarah J. Koppel, for always embracing me in love.

1 Playfully Misfit

A Vision for Effective Pastoral Leadership

> I [Lady Wisdom] was next to him like an artisan. I was a delight
> day by day rejoicing before him for all time, rejoicing in his inhabited
> world, and delighting in humankind.
>
> —Proverbs 8:30-31

An encounter with a child in a beloved biblical narrative provides an image of *open-hearted ministry*. In John's account of Jesus feeding the five thousand, a little boy offers the five loaves and two fish to feed the crowd of hungry people gathered around Jesus on a mountain. Discussion between Jesus and the disciples is rendered in this way:

> Jesus said to Philip, "Where are we to buy bread for these people to eat?" He said this to test him, for he himself knew what he was going to do. Philip answered him, "Six months' wages would not buy enough bread for each of them to get a little." One of his disciples, Andrew, Simon Peter's brother, said to him, *"There is a boy here who has five barley loaves and two fish. But what are they among so many people?"* Jesus said, "Make the people sit down." (John 6:5-10) [Emphasis added.]

A *child* provides the barley loaves and fish; this gesture stirs the soul. The image captures a deep adulthood longing: to offer a willing, timely, and generous gift to God, resources that can be used to feed many hungry people.

This scriptural passage sparks the imagination even as it raises questions: Does the child offer the loaves and fish on his own? Does an older family member nudge him to offer the provisions of the family? Regardless, the gesture of the little boy is emotionally stirring because it touches the spirit of the child within us who seeks to offer to God a gift of generosity from the heart that can be beneficial for all.

We make such offering willingly in spite of the ways of the world: people hoard valuable resources; institutions can function to keep some hungry while others have plenty; people harden their hearts to the needy while surrounded by bounty and plenty. Symbolized as a child, the spirit of generosity dwells within all of us and seeks expression, a spark in a world dimmed with greed.

Symbolized as a child, the spirit of generosity dwells within all of us and seeks expression, a spark in a world dimmed with greed.

A child, one who is considered among the least of society, carries provisions that satisfy the hunger of many people. The gospel account turns expectations upside down: sustenance comes from a previously unimaginable source. So, too, this book intends to reframe expectations of ourselves and our practices in ministry by inviting pastoral leaders to claim a valuable resource: neglected parts of themselves and others, their misfit nature. *Misfit* refers to persons, qualities, and experiences that do not correspond to dominant perspectives. The term "misfit" names an identity that needs to be reclaimed and celebrated. "Healthy misfits" include pastors and congregations who express *vitality*, the "essential aliveness and life-affirmation, ... human agency that manifests in passion and capacity to endure,"[1] and devote themselves to life-affirming and life-fostering practices. By "healthy misfits" I am not referring to those who have assimilated, and therefore negated, valuable characteristics. My seminary mentor, the late Professor Letty M. Russell, often spoke of herself as one of God's misfits. Letty graduated from Harvard Divinity School with honors in an era when few women attended seminary. One of the first women ordained in the Presbyterian Church, Letty served for many years as a parish minister in East Harlem and professor of theology at Yale Divinity School.

Letty's passionate gifts of teaching, preaching, writing, and community organizing influenced a generation of leaders and lay people. As advocate for marginalized persons, Letty sought to change ecclesial structures and organizations in order to make room for all God's beloved people.

> **Definition: misfit. Misfit refers to persons, qualities, and experiences that do not correspond to dominant perspectives.**

Healthy misfits are those who are able to negotiate relationally the creative tension of being different and are able to invite others to do the same. These overlooked and frequently derided aspects are unique gifts and skills that God has sown within each of us to be shared in community, a resource for creative and playful servant leadership. Through honoring the gifts of effective misfit pastoral leadership, we, like the child in John's gospel, offer to God valuable resources that can help satisfy hungry souls.   *ImPRoV!*

Pastoral leadership requires both the maturity and agility symbolic of adulthood and the open-spirited generosity symbolic of childhood. Many people enter ministry with hearts, minds, and hands joyously eager to respond to God's call to serve the church and the cries of a hungry and hurting world. Yet we may grow weary of all the responsibilities and tasks that beckon. All too often it seems as if there are not enough hours in any given week to accomplish all that we set out to do. Sometimes the resistance we encounter, whether it is within our own souls or in relationship with others or within our institutions, can leave us depleted, worn-out, and tired. We may second-guess ourselves, question the motives of others, and feel burdened by the weight of all that looms before us.

In this book, I invite readers *to own their sense of being a misfit* in order to engage more playfully and creatively in ministry. This sense of being a misfit comes in many ways: we may be introverted or extroverted, young or old, women or men, first career, second career or even third career ministers. Whatever the circumstance, when we realize that our ministry is not like everyone else's or that we are different from other ministers in some way, we might assume that a difference in character and behavior is the result of a flaw. Making changes on the assumption that something is wrong with us or the community may result in confusion and frustration, while to owning our misfit allows us to claim and affirm the value of marginality and difference since its presence is valuable for ministry in God's church. When we own a disregarded or neglected aspect of ourselves or our communities, recognizing its importance and significance, then we are free to employ our unique gifts in service to others.

Valuing difference in ourselves, in other people, and in our congregations is one key aspect of owning misfit nature. The challenge is to become fully the people and the communities that God is calling us to be. In the many splendorous nuances of this variety, God surely delights. When ministers and congregations own their misfit nature by offering diverse gifts, then everyone shares in the resulting synergistic abundance, as the story from John's gospel captures.

Creativity and play are not additional "tasks" that we have to put on a checklist to accomplish. Play is not yet another thing we have to become better at in order to develop excellence in ministry. The capacity for play and creativity, rather, are inherently within us; we cannot help but to be playful and creative when the conditions are right. This book invites you to be the playful, creative, misfit leader God has chosen you to be; it also invites misfit church communities to celebrate their own unique calling in God's realm. When we own our misfit qualities and characteristics, we open ourselves to the movement of the Holy Spirit that lives in relation to all creation, awakening and calling us forth to abundant and fruitful life.

The Difficulty of Play

Play refers to meaningful thought and behavior that has pattern to it without being completely prescribed or pre-determined. Play may at times take the form of frivolous action. Play may also be a form of purposeful thought and behavior through which we relate to others and the environment. Consider the playful practices of a campus pastor and a church administrator. Rev. John, focused on creating a new chapel for the ministry, invited college students to help design a worship space. Through the students' free-form interaction with one another and in collaboration with Rev. John, the final design took on a completely different configuration than the pastor could have originally imagined. By hanging loose with the process and staying in touch with the students' desires, Rev. John embodied a playful spirit. The prayer chapel became precisely what the community wanted and needed.

Relieved by the Bishop from duties as a church administrator, Pastor Jane felt betrayed for speaking her convictions and suggesting new directions for ministry. During a time of painful transition, she found solace in the practice of making quilts, a creative release for her gift of imagination. While interviewing for a position in a local congregation, Rev. Jane knew that she had finally returned home as she noticed the quilted paraments on the altar. Through this solitary practice, Rev. Jane creatively played her way into a new place in ministry.

Definition: play. *Play refers to meaningful thought and behavior—sometimes frivolous, sometimes purposeful—that has pattern to it without being completely prescribed or pre-determined.*

Play is not easy for many adults. Many of us have deeply engrained messages about the way we are supposed to behave, and being playful is usually not one of them. Why is play so difficult?

- We often have thoughts of work going through our minds. We carry a mental and actual checklist of all the things we have to do in the short-term and long-term. Play can be difficult because, ironically enough, we derive pleasure from work, especially when it brings accolades from parishioners and colleagues. When work is not going well, though, we might try to remedy the situation by working even harder, thereby exacerbating stress.

Play — Rooted in Identity as well as a vocation

- We more often associate our identities with work and productivity than with play and being. Many of us regularly adopt this misguided assumption. We are, in fact, beloved creatures of God in play and in work. In so far as we only hitch our identities to constant productivity and accomplishment, we will be sorely disappointed, angry at ourselves even, when we don't get much done.

- We like to think of ourselves as purposeful, rather than purposeless, in our ministries. We are accustomed to making good use of time and resources. We can relegate practice of play, or any conceptions of it, to a luxury at best and a waste of time at worst.

embrace inner fool

- We tend to minimize play both personally and culturally. We may endorse the value of play for other people, while secretly we harbor doubts about it for ourselves. We may believe ourselves to be incompetent at play or may fear appearing childish or foolish. We'd rather not have people think of us, and may not like to think of ourselves, as childish.

- We have trouble releasing personal and social constraints. Play, especially when there are few explicit rules and lots of unknowns, can be unsettling for adults. We generally like to think we know what we're doing; and those we lead would like to know that we know what we're doing. We fear being seen as incompetent or impostors.

- We do not necessarily believe that pleasure and enjoyment can be a part of satisfying ministry. We may flog ourselves internally with nagging messages of negative self-worth, or work ourselves to exhaustion before we can permit ourselves to play. Unfortunately, we communicate this message — that pain must precede play — unwittingly to others as long as we believe it to be true ourselves.

- We may hurry to premature judgment. We find play difficult because we want to see material results from our playing. Play is difficult because we turn it into another "self-improvement" or "improvement of others" project. In short, we want play to work for us. ✷✷

✷✷ [Creative play is really a posture of the soul, an alignment of willful intention and bodily presence.] In genuine play, we show up in ministry—body, mind, and spirit—aware of the well-being or lack thereof in the lives of others. In genuine play, we do not dismiss or slight others, but rather bring a wakeful and rested presence, ready to interact with people and to engage in tasks wholeheartedly, allowing ourselves and others to alternate between moments of levity and seriousness.

Uniting Head and Heart in Ministry

Playful practice in ministry is embodied pastoral theology. The experience of creativity emerges at the intersection of the mature and the childlike, a place where wisdom and awe, intentionality, as well as serendipity can meet. We embody this theology as we unite the head and heart in the service of ministry.

Charles Wesley's phrase inscribed on the library cornerstone at Wesley Seminary serves as reminder of this integrative work: Unite the pair so long disjoin'd, Knowledge and vital piety. The architecture of the school conveys symbolically the value of uniting the head and heart: large windows of the library's main reading room are situated directly across a courtyard from large windows revealing the main chapel. The structure of the buildings enshrines the dynamic interplay of scholarship and living faith. As an embodied theology, play enables pastoral leaders to integrate a vital and passionate faith, a keen and searching intellect, and a well-honed ability to engage interpersonally. The ability to draw on these various sources, with different emphasis depending on the context, is itself a form of creative play. The harmonious linking of head and heart produces a synergistic abundance of energy. We tap into the deep reservoir of God's Spirit and may be surprised by the results.

This embodied theology that honors the dynamic interplay of head and heart, of rationality and intuition, can surprise ministers in many ways. We write a sermon for Sunday worship, carefully crafted for the appointed Scripture of the day, only to have a crisis erupt that requires a radical shift in our attention. We drop the planned sermon and speak extemporaneously. Or as a hospital chaplain, we carefully chart a spiritual care plan for a long-term patient, but eventually let go of the plan to be fully present with whatever occurs in the moment. These are not capricious decisions; they are intentional, informed, and wise. The extra reservoir in this embodied theology may emerge just as we get to the edge of an experience and want to abandon the established plan altogether. We have pushed something as far as we can, and then we let go. Something entirely new is free to emerge. We stand out of the way and let God's creative energy abound. Even though we may not be aware of it in the moment, we later glimpse God at play in the situation.

We need to tell stories about creative play and play practices in ministry because this is one way to capture God's activity in the world. Personal narrative and experience has a place in theology. Jung Young Lee, a Korean-American theologian, clarifies the purpose of personal experience: "Theology is autobiographical, but it is not autobiography."[2] Play is autobiographical in the sense that it reflects the nuances and complexity of our personalities; parishioners and congregants want to hear stories of how to value play in their faith lives. Yet in telling these stories, we are not crafting an autobiography that sets us apart from others, but referencing how we encounter the God of life in our playing. Play as embodied theology values being *responsive to* intuition as well as intellect and also *responsible for* fulfillment of obligations and commitments. Play, as a theology of leadership, contributes to a desire to engage in ethical and creative play in ministry.

The Difference Play Makes

Play as embodied theology puts us in touch with the natural rhythm of life. We become more attuned to what needs to happen when, instead of forcing things or placing our agenda on them, we allow them to unfold naturally. Though difficult, play can prove beneficial for ministry in the following ways.

Sensible strategies. Timelines and plans allow us to restore or maintain energy and balance in our communities. Sensible strategies may mean letting go of timelines and deadlines, even temporarily, so that new insights and practices can emerge. The process runs counter to our usual sensibility.

> At the behest of the associate pastor, a local church decided to start a small group congregational care ministry. This proved to be a good idea with not-so-good timing. The church already had many smaller group ministries that functioned self-sufficiently. Through honest and sensitive conversation with key church leaders, the associate pastor in conversation with the senior minister and the coordinating committee eventually decided that temporary suspension of starting the new groups might make a difference. The postponement allowed the congregation to experience a reinvestment of energy in the already existing ministries.

Allow not-knowing to be a guide rather than a hindrance. One fallacy often gets in the way of ministerial leaders: thinking we need to know the answers or a predetermined outcome when we don't actually know. Seminary students in beginning pastoral care courses often are eager to learn the skills and techniques that can initiate care programs and respond meaningfully to hurting people in congregation and community. Some want to know the precise steps they should take in any given situation. It can be unsettling for them to hear that "not-knowing" can be a valuable stance.

> **"When I don't know something, I am more likely to be curious and open-minded—it's like I'm learning right along with the other person"** . . . Allowing not-knowing to be our guide is another way of saying that we have to get ourselves out of the way enough for God's authentic healing and wisdom to emerge.

Even experienced pastoral leaders want to hone the skills and techniques to do ministry the so-called right way. A gathering of ministers seeking advanced degrees, many of them with years of experience, have gradually come to realize that what they don't know can be as valuable as what they do. One leader comments, "When I don't know something, I am more likely to be curious and open-minded—it's like I'm learning right along with the other person." Of course, well-developed listening and attending skills are indispensable for pastoral leaders and caregivers. Equally important, though, is the cultivated quality of presence that accompanies skill that proves beneficial for helping others. Remaining in this space of not-knowing can be an un-settling experience. Gradually, with the exercise of patience, we realize that a playful spirit enables us to stay in the not-knowing with our-selves and others. We don't move herky-jerky expecting ourselves to create solutions for everything. Play as a process of resting more com-fortably in the unknown helps build the confidence that allows not-knowing, in a sense, to become our teacher. Allowing not-knowing to be our guide is another way of saying that we have to get ourselves out of the way enough for God's authentic healing and wisdom to emerge.

Play helps to contain anxiety and guilt. In the long-run, guilt-driven or anxiety-driven ministry is not beneficial for congregations or their leaders. Play as an intentional means of serving God and others actually creates a container for anxiety and guilt. We live in a time when many people are burdened with the anxiety of caring for aging parents while raising children, fulfilling work demands, generating enough income to make ends meet, and so on. Some level of stress keeps us awake in our ministries, and attentive to mission in our midst. Too much anxi-ety overwhelms the individual and collective spirit causing everyone to wither. Anxiety over our own shortcomings often leads to feelings of guilt. The capacity to feel guilt means that we have the ability to make a difference, to act responsibly when the anxiety arises. Yet taking too much responsibility as a way to control our feelings of guilt—such as micromanaging every aspect of congregational life—is detrimental to everyone's health.

Play helps to bring elasticity to anxiety and guilt. We gain perspec-tive to see with clarity. The insight of Reinhold Niebuhr's Serenity prayer is appropriate: "God grant us the serenity to accept the things we cannot change, courage to change the things we can, and wisdom to know the difference." Play as embodied theology helps to contain anxiety and guilt so that we can maintain contact with our inherent flexibility and resilience.

Play develops from taking small steps. Actually, play celebrates in small steps. We don't always need to make big projects out of our lives or our ministries. Learning to take small steps can be immensely gratifying. The Zen Buddhist practice of meditative walking (called *kinhin*) is illustrative. This practice focuses the mind as intently and fully as possible on walking sensations, feeling the foot's pressure on the ground, and the movement of muscles and bones. This spiritual practice is a means to stay fully engaged in the moment and to become more aware of what we actually miss in our environment. Live fully in the small steps.   *incrementality*

Creative play revels in taking small steps. A group from a church governing body gathered one Sunday evening for conversation and play. They decided to take up a game of badminton; as the sun set and evening turned to night, they played. Their game did not follow any of the usual rules of badminton. With two on each side of the net, they experienced delight in simply keeping the birdie in the air. Competition to defeat an opponent was transformed into a playful challenge to continue the volleys. The goal increased as the number of back and forth hits rose. The community spirit that developed through this dynamic was sheer fun. Everyone emerged as a winner through the small step of transforming a game.

Consciously finding ways to keep people in play, with even the smallest of steps, is itself success in ministry.

Play helps to reign in the all-too-prevalent tendency to "fix" situations. Certainly we want to help people, but what we imagine to be helpful may not be. Our urge to "fix" another person arises when something about them or their situation *makes us* uncomfortable. We dislike the internal discomfort *we feel* in their presence. Play as embodied

FIX NOT
✗

theology allows us to accept discomfort and become a more available presence without the need to offer a solution.

Creative Pastoral Leadership

As pastoral leaders, God calls us to become authentically who we are in dynamic tension with the environment in which we minister. Creative religious leadership stands within the tension of conformity, on the one side, and idiosyncrasy, on the other. The ability to navigate this tension is a dilemma for many faithful people and communities. At the heart of the matter is how best to foster vibrancy in ministry. *A certain level of being misfit is necessary for creative and productive leadership.*

In our efforts to conform, personally as well as collectively, we often overlook, contain, or get rid of misfits — persons, qualities, and experiences — that do not adhere to our preconceptions. We may disdain the misfit nature of other people because we dislike, and may wish to disown, the misfit nature in ourselves. We deny the value of marginality, the phenomenon of creative negotiation between worlds of experience, whether this occurs *within* ourselves or *between* ourselves and other people. We generally tend to manipulate, and re-form that which appears different in our midst. We resist misfitness pervasively on personal, social, and institutional levels.

How does marginality relate to pastoral leadership? Marginality, of course, is a term that defines an aspect in relation to something else: marginality is measured in comparison to a certain standard. Play influences two aspects of marginality: the ability to lead creatively as a marginal person (for example being a woman in ministry) and the ability to lead a marginal institution (for example the church in relation to the wider culture). These two types of marginality, in my view, are interrelated. The institution which is marginal itself marginalizes members and leaders. One study finds that the *marginality of organized religion* itself may deter people from religious leadership.[3] Yet, marginalized people bring gifts and skills for negotiating personal and social dynamics that can be of benefit to the entire community.

As misfit pastoral leaders embrace the reality of this double tension—marginal people within an already marginal institution—we may experience the freedom to engage creative and playful qualities in the practice of ministry, including: curiosity, spontaneity, passion,compassion, initiation, as well as the ability to lead with the head, the heart, and instinct.[4] Let's consider the story of a pastoral leader who has claimed and celebrated her own marginality.

Josephine's Story

Josephine Pratt was orphaned at a young age when a tragic car accident left her and her sister without parents. In spite of the hardship of her early life, Josephine married and had several children. She heeded her call to ministry later in life, after having reared a family and enduring a painful divorce from her husband. Yet while in seminary, she found a spiritual home in a congregation with a significant outreach to the homeless in the city. As an educated southern woman, previously married, and a cancer survivor, Josephine also had tremendous gifts as an artist.

She pursued the ordination track in her denomination only to be told by the bishop that ordination was in question because "there was not enough space for her" in the diocese. Josephine sensed that the bishop did not know what to do with her. Insightful, artistic, vivacious, warm, welcoming, and expressive of her feelings, Josephine did not "fit" the image of her denomination's typical southern church pastor. The bishop told her that there probably would not be a ministry match for her in the diocese.

Josephine grieved the loss of a vision toward which she felt God calling her: to celebrate the sacraments, preach, teach, and care for God's people. She grieved, but did not give up hope. In typical Josephine style, she declared that she would pursue other means to help mend the world and tend to hurting souls. She knew that there was much she could contribute, perhaps in another denomination or as a lay minister in her own, even if she were not ordained. Saddened by the turn of events, and with private moments of grief,

Josephine toyed with plans for the future. The experience surfaced feelings of isolation, abandonment, and loss reminiscent of losing her parents in childhood, and of divorcing her husband and struggling as a cancer survivor in adulthood. Josephine didn't soldier on, but she did "play on." She laughed and celebrated, while still respecting the authority of the church council and the bishop. She played by responding to events and making plans in a way that sustained her soul. Josephine readily embraces the identity of misfit. Others sometimes don't know what to do with her, but God does.

Eventually, the bishop changed his mind and decided that Josephine was, in fact, suited for ministry. It was an outer confirmation of a long process that had brought her to this point. Today she serves as an ordained leader in a parish in her denomination.

Focus of the Book

Play exercised in the practice of ministry equips misfit ministers to lead effectively. There are various dimensions to "healthy misfits" involving experiences, qualities, and persons. As misfit ministers live deeply into marginality, we discover new dimensions of vocation and shape the church's ministry in valuable ways.

Let's consider a definition of play to guide the practice of ministry. Play as embodied theology:

- is cooperative engagement *within the self* and *between self and others* that heightens enjoyment of God and pulls us more deeply into life experience.

- incorporates the new and innovative within already structured patterns of behavior.

- allows for making mistakes as we develop creative, and sometimes previously unimagined, pastoral leadership practices.[5]

As embodied pastoral theology, play can be defined as structuring chaos. Structuring chaos means that we relate intentionally, meaningfully, emotionally, and skillfully, in varying measure and according to our personality, even as we are aware of many possible outcomes. Structuring chaos is an active rather than a passive process. Some may think of play only as fun and frivolous, but it actually represents an attunement to the environment, other people, and ourselves, freeing us intellectually and emotionally to unleash energy already present.

> *Some may think of play only as fun and frivolous, but it actually represents an attunement to the environment, other people, and ourselves, freeing us intellectually and emotionally to unleash energy already present.*

Ministry can often feel more chaotic than orderly, and maybe that's the way it should be. James Dittes, pastoral theologian at Yale for more than forty years, writes that ministry is "intended to be a *chronic misfit*, comfortable resident of neither heaven nor earth because committed — like the persistent God who calls — to *reconcile these irreconcilable domains*."[6] Structuring chaos is another way of naming this misfit work of "reconciling the irreconcilable domains of heaven and earth." Know that this work will not be complete in our lifetimes, and the perception of chaos does not indicate ineffectiveness. Effective pastoral leadership requires us to minister creatively and constructively in the midst of changing circumstances to help facilitate vitality for individuals and communities in contexts that balance structure with chaos.

I invite readers to reconsider their own perspective on creative pastoral leadership and imagine room for play in theology and practices.[7] Play may be a means to sustain our vitality as healthy, fairly well-adjusted misfits in ministry. When people ask me what I am passionate about in ministry, I respond by saying, "I am passionate about play in ministry!"

Through play, which includes taking ourselves less seriously at times, we begin to sense God's presence. Pastoral leadership and play are not merely about the repetition of the predictable but involve encounter with the unknown and the unpredictable. In play, we meet God, who is Mystery.

Ethical Pastoral Play

Pastoral leaders, perhaps more so than other people in the helping professions, have the challenge of being intimate with people in various contexts while also maintaining clear and appropriate professional boundaries. Play is one way to think about negotiating the tension in maintaining the boundaries while restructuring them. Pastoral leaders who have had doorway conversations with parishioners about personal matters know the delicate balance of listening to the confidences of people while also staying mindful of a conversation's public context. Engaging effectively and creatively in this environment is a playful endeavor.

Play as an embodied theology can contribute to health and healing, for persons and for congregations, to the degree that it is grounded in the professional and ethical principles to which we need to be held accountable.[8] Ethical engagement with play helps pastoral leaders exercise responsibility in addition to creative leadership.

An ethic frames, shapes, and contains play so that it contributes to well-being for all and limits the possibility for play's misuse. My own ethic of play is guided by a Christian theological vision that God calls all people and communities to abundant and fruitful life. Ethical play leads to the support and increase of resilience, faithfulness, commitment, and love between persons and within communities.

The *principled and ethical use of play in the ministry* adheres to specified criteria, against which potentially life-giving play may be held accountable. Ethical play creates a defined physical and attitudinal space that honors complexity and diversity. Ethical play allows for creative difference between people and facilitates an open perspective to experience one's self and that of others. Ethical play allows for the expression of new behavior patterns that respect the concerns of tradition

safe space

and professional standards. Ethical play supports the experience and awareness of deeply felt emotion that may be appropriately expressed depending on contextual circumstances. Ethical play increases resilience and fosters faith.

I Get the Point — So Why Read the Entire Book?!

A ministerial colleague once sheepishly admitted that he rarely reads books beyond the first chapter. "I am embarrassed to admit it — but those who buy my previously owned books at the rummage sale will know — I don't always read past the introduction. I figure I get the point of the argument so why bother seeing how it will be fleshed out and repeated throughout the rest of the chapters." Many of us, whether or not we openly acknowledge it, share the sentiment of this colleague. We want to get to the point of the book or article quickly because our time is limited; many demands press upon us. So in the spirit of play, I invite you to skip around. Read what interests you and sparks your imagination for ministry, and leave the rest. I share my vision for pastoral ministry to help you deepen and develop beneficial practices in your context.

I realized that the topic had a history, even if it was not delineated as such. Prophets, disciples, nomadic people wandering in the desert, and a baby born in a manger bed are all representative of valuable misfits. God's cast of characters is a motley crew. The Protestant reformers, such as Martin Luther, were misfits who called for change. Misfits are compelling figures precisely because they are unique. My own ministerial experiences have been quite diverse, including many "misfit" experiences that shaped and formed my own pastoral identity. Other people who heed the call to ministry, I suspect, may have their own misfit experiences. Creative ministries depend on pastoral leaders who are willing to risk failure as well as success. Incorporating play into ministry and embracing misfitness is a form of risk-taking, or what Page Smith calls "the demonstration of courage."[9]

Playful pastoral leadership seeks to be faithful to the gospel message. This open–hearted style of ministry equally values the ability to laugh and to cry, to celebrate and to mourn, to pray and to play.

Playful pastoral leadership seeks to be faithful to the gospel message. This open-hearted style of ministry equally values the ability to laugh and to cry, to celebrate and to mourn, to pray and to play. Like the often overlooked child in John's gospel, creative misfit leaders and communities offer gifts that God uses to heal and to feed an often hurting and hungry world.

Questions for Personal and Group Reflection

1. Reflect on the image of the little boy in John's gospel. What do you imagine it's like to be this child in Jesus' presence? What does this child represent for you? What does the child's gesture prompt in you?

2. In what ways are you or your community "misfits"? To what extent are you able to "own" this misfit nature? What values, perspectives, or qualities do misfits contribute to God's church?

3. What is your definition of theological play? What thoughts or beliefs interfere with your ability to play? What thoughts or beliefs support creative play?

4. Tell or write the story of your own call to ministry as a lay person or as a pastoral leader? What "misfit" aspects — humorous, unanticipated, or nonsensical — get left out of the story because you fear others may not believe you?

5. Imagine a creative or play-filled practice for ministry. Name the first step that can be taken to embody this vision.

6. Reflect on a dream for ministry in your context. Identify the anxieties and hopes embedded in this vision.

7. How has energy been drained in your community's ministry? What can be implemented to re-direct the mission?

8. What is the dominant image of God for your congregation? What is a central image for you? Identify the creative tensions in the differences.

9. How would you define marginal or misfit people? What is your history as a misfit and/or with ministering to marginalized people?

10. In what ways can authority figures support play? How can they interfere with play?

2 Play and Grief
Renewing Trust for Ministry

Life is a good teacher and a good friend. Things are always in tran-
sition, if we could only realize it. Nothing ever sums itself up in the
way that we like to dream about it. The off-center, in-between state
is an ideal situation, a situation in which we don't get caught and
we can open our hearts and minds beyond limit. It's a very tender,
nonaggressive, open-ended state of affairs.

— Pema Chodron
When Things Fall Apart

Wesley Theological Seminary sits on a slight hill next to American University on one of the main avenues in a primarily residential neighborhood in Washington, D.C. Ordinarily, people comment that they didn't know the school was even there because the buildings blend into the hillside. The slope of grass leading up to the buildings is a prominent feature of the terrain. On the evening of All Saints' Day in 2005 that hillside became a site of remembrance that poignantly combined grief and play.

Preparation started on the previous day. Dozens of people, in a spirit of playful conviviality, placed sand in the bottom of white paper bags and put a candle in each bag. They then placed the bags along the slope, lined up in row that filled the hillside. Some people came only to help for a brief period as their schedules permitted. Others came to help, left to fulfill other obligations, and then returned to continue the project. A few worked steadily throughout the day. Woven throughout all the preparation was a sense of community, a gathering of people working cooperatively and imaginatively toward a common vision. A spirit of playful camaraderie was present among the folks working on the project. But something else brought them to this occasion: a sense of grief and sadness.

Early in the evening of All Saints Day the candles were lit, one for each American service man or woman killed in Iraq, then a group gathered at the bottom of the hill for a Service of Remembrance. We prayed for all the saints, including all these soldiers and the civilians who have died during this time of war. Through the prayers, readings and songs of the liturgy, the people expressed grief and remembered those who are gone.

The flickering light of more than two thousand candles on a hillside was arresting and soul-moving. Cars slowed down and people walking along the street stopped in respectful reverence. Perhaps they were just curious or perhaps they, too, were captivated by the sight as well as the grief and sadness that stirred within. From a distance these candles of remembrance could be (mis)taken for cemetery gravestones: markers of lives whose play has ended.

Play and Grief in Ministry

Play and grief together can inform our practices in ministry. We might initially think that "off-center" and "in-between" describe an unhealthy and doomed ministry. We will explore how just the opposite is usually true. The ability to negotiate relationally the "in-between space" contributes to lively and creative ministry.[1] The complex emotion of grief is an especially good example of negotiating this space because as we recognize and accept it we can bring a renewed sense of purpose and trust to ministry. Deep and authentic grieving can open internal space to allow for creativity and play in surprisingly new ways. Grieving is a psychological indication that we are releasing attachment to someone or something and opening ourselves to the "next thing."[2] Grief, often considered antithetical to play, can also be the opening of our hearts to play.

We don't always begin with flourishing in the ministry. Usually an experience of disappointment, dissatisfaction, or failure prompts us to try something new. Being new and serious to our task, we don't feel able to play. The experience of not-playing, or loss of enjoyment, begins to gnaw and slowly a new awareness emerges. Although we may start the spiritual journey of pastoral leadership with a true desire to love God, we end up, instead, pleasing and conforming to the desires of other people. The true and authentic desire, in other words, gives way to something that can seem artificial and contrived. Over time, we may feel ourselves becoming more wooden and manipulated.

Ministry at the margins is a metaphor to describe a pattern of relationship with other people and within systems that do not place our own ego needs as central. To flourish at the margins is to know and experience God's love and vitality at the center of existence. Creative "off-balance" in ministry is mostly about focusing attention on God's activity in our midst. As leaders we embrace marginality because we recognize at the deepest level of our souls the importance of teaching others to serve God, the Center and Source of All Being. In play we revel in God as the Center of Existence and let go of the need to be the center ourselves.

Standing at the margins as pastoral leaders and communities teaches us valuable lessons. We participate in what the authors of one study call the "constructive, enlarging engagement with the other" beyond the concerns of our particular "tribe" or grouping.[3] We learn to care for people and aspects of creation that are different from ourselves as we realize that we are connected to the whole of God's creation. All the parts are intimately and intricately connected. We offer hospitality to the stranger and friend alike because we recognize what it's like to feel less valued standing at the margins as "the other" or the outsider.[4] And there is a distinct social benefit from the experience of being a marginal person within a system or institution: positioning oneself at the "edge of one's tribe or society appears to contribute to the ability to move between tribes."[5] Misfit ministers who recognize and celebrate their own marginality help marginal persons "interpret difference in positive ways."[6] We are led to fulfill the gospel call to respond with compassion and care to the needs of the "stranger next door" because we are sensitive to their struggles and concerns.

Flourishing in Pastoral Ministry: From Normalcy to Vitality

How do we describe psychological and spiritual well-being in pastoral leadership? Let's consider the benefits and disadvantages of three different descriptors (as well as how we use them to interpret ministry, including ourselves and our communities): normal, healthy, and vital. Play encourages us to move beyond normal and healthy, both of which can be achieved without embracing our inner misfit. Play allows us to tolerate the tensions of creative misfitting in order to live fully into vitality of mind and heart.

- Normal is a term that measures one aspect in comparison to another and encompasses a fairly limited number of patterns. We usually determine normal in relationship to its opposite: the abnormal. Normalcy can be a problematic term when used to describe human beings and communities because it does not sufficiently account for positive complexity of experience and diversity in relationship patterns. We measure "normal" against some objective standard. What, though, does a "normal" congregation look like?

- Health generally refers to the absence of pathology. We would probably describe a "healthy" minister or congregation as one that functions well with relatively few problems. Leaders and communities sometimes maintain health by not conforming to the expectations of others. It can be a mark of psychological and spiritual health actually to confront the typical way of doing things rather than conform to them. Health can be inversely related to conformity. Healthy leaders and communities are usually free to minister creatively, and are willing to take more risks.

- Vitality, like flourishing, describes an "essential aliveness and life-affirmation, . . . human agency that manifests in passion and capacity to endure."[7] We use "vital" to describe people and communities who have lots of vibrant energy. They seem to be living for all the right reasons. Vitality emerges from living intentionally to the experience and fulfillment of abundant life. Flourishing and abundant life are Divine gifts that we do not create ourselves. Rather we open ourselves to the experience of those gifts. Vitality is also connected to health and well-being. Pastoral leaders and communities can live healthy yet not abundant lives.[8] We thrive in ministry as we step beyond health and well-being. Play, in its many forms, nurtures vitality and helps people and congregations to flourish. Play can nourish us even when health and well-being are threatened.

Reclaiming Emotions in Pastoral Leadership

Let's look at one way to make a "space" for marginal experience in ministry, and thus tap a reservoir of vitality. Emotions themselves are a part of misfit experience that needs to be reclaimed and integrated. In a scientific and technological age that values rationality, we often live cut off from the depth of our feelings and emotions. It may seem a good thing not to work with the "difficult" emotions of anger, rage, and fear; but we are also cut off from the depth of other feelings and emotions such as joy, elation, and happiness. When pastoral leaders push aside an entire realm of emotional experience, ministry can become superficial, out-of-touch, and unsatisfying for everyone.

We ignore emotions at our own peril. Emotions are "the misfit" as long as we think of the rational intellect as the superior function. Dynamic and vital ministry needs mature emotional awareness as well as keen intellectual skills. We do well to consider thinking and feeling as complementary rather than diametrically opposed functions.[9] Emotions are intelligent in part because they tell us something about how and who we are. At times, we are able to control our emotions, and at others they seem to arise spontaneously without our intention. Knowing this interplay of emotions within — when we feel in control of our emotions and when they seem to be in control of us—helps ministers become less fearful of emotional complexity. While we might not initially fully understand the meaning of our own or other people's emotions, we may be more open simply to listening.

Grief is often a misfit emotion for religious leaders and communities. We don't quite know what to "do" with it. Grief carries intelligence, though, as it wakes the soul to depth and significance; we let go, however reluctantly and painfully, of attachments of old ways of doing things. Without this process, our feelings and emotions remain dormant, possibly leading to psychic and social distress. As we learn to recognize the contours of grief, and to accept and even to embrace its presence, we help to foster vitality in others and ourselves.

Grieving is a central piece of emotional work.[10] Attention to the grief process attunes pastoral leaders and caregivers to the state of their own emotional lives. We encounter a range of emotions, including feelings of loss and anger as well as joy and gratitude. We grieve ways in which we have not played and reveled in God's creation. We grieve over the time spent on tasks that divert our attention from the important matters of ministry. Carefully secured within the process of grief is deep remembrance of a stored image, of the experience of what God continually calls us to be. Grief is therefore significant for emotional life because it reminds us of this *imago Dei,* our deep connection to God and to one another. When we ignore grief, we refuse on some level to participate in life. Alternatively, through grief we are able to open ourselves and our communities to a renewed vitality and the reflection of divine grace fully alive in the world.

Carefully secured within the process of grief is deep remembrance of a stored image, of the experience of what God continually calls us to be. Grief is therefore significant for emotional life because it reminds us of this imago Dei.

Ignoring grief can have adverse effects. If we do not care for grief, it can lead to deep psychological depression. The process of living is stopped, in effect, by a refusal, whether conscious or unconscious, to acknowledge experiences of pain and loss. Depression can be, though is not always, a result of this refusal. An inability to acknowledge and express grief carries with it also the possible effect of disconnection from, or repression of, vitality. Those unwilling or unable to grieve may need the assistance of a skilled professional.

Pastoral leaders regularly touch pain in the experience of others. Personal grief may be triggered by and become entangled with the grief of care receivers. Ignoring this grief makes us less effective care givers, susceptible to depression, and prone to higher degrees of irritability and restlessness. This may contribute, in part, to the living out of what Kathleen Greider refers to as "violent aggression."[11] Instead of reacting to situations with flexibility and resilience, we find ourselves lashing out in harmful and destructive ways. Attending to the process of grief diminishes the likelihood that we respond to others with immature or unhealthy aggression.

The separation of emotions from our spiritual life and practices can be harmful to us and to those entrusted to our care. This harm, in some cases, might have detrimental and irreversible relational effects. Such is the case when pastoral leaders, disconnected from their own psychological and emotional needs, violate physical and emotional boundaries with parishioners or students. Pastoral leaders therefore have the capacity to scar deeply the lives of the faithful.

Effective pastoral leadership benefits from a skilled understanding of rational and emotional intelligence. Emotional intelligence,[12] as an essential element in creative and playful pastoral ministry, can be fostered in a number of ways.

- *Knowing one's emotions.* As we know ourselves emotionally, so we are more likely to feel in control of what we are doing, and also to know our limits. When we recognize grief, we allow the process to occur without the need to "stop it" or "get rid of it." We simply pay attention to the feelings, bringing awareness and compassion to what we find.

- *Managing emotions.* Emotionally intelligent pastoral leaders are capable of expressing emotions when necessary and will refrain from that expression when inappropriate. We make conscious choices about what we do with the feelings. When a pastoral activity triggers the grief process in this regard, we make a mental note of it and, at an appropriate time, create a space for listening to the grief in our own hearts.

- *Motivating oneself.* Acknowledging grief is an emotionally intelligent practice because it can be a powerful means for charting new directions in ministry. Pastoral leaders trained for interim ministry are keenly aware of this and are skilled to help congregations motivate themselves through times of transition. A sense of listlessness in a congregation may then be transformed into a renewed focus on ministry and mission.

- *Recognizing emotions in others.* Emotional intelligence is only partly about knowing our own lives of feeling and emotion. The larger purpose of this important internal work is to sensitize pastoral leaders to inner lives of other people. If we recognize the difficulty of expressing emotion, we are sensitive to how others may have difficulty. If we know the tendency to rationalize or intellectualize an emotion, we are sensitive to this tendency in others. Through the practice of watching our own emotions, we are more alert to their presence (or absence) in others.

- *Handling relationships.* Pastoral leaders engage in grief work of their own in an effort to foster what one author calls "interpathy."[13] This is the learned skill of being able to extend empathy and compassion toward others, no matter how difficult their experience of grieving or loss. Personal grief work makes pastoral leaders less fearful of the varied grief processes of other people. Allowing for the presence of grief and other deeply felt emotions in ministry gives breadth and depth to the community relationships. People and communities that allow for real and authentic grief cultivate groundwork for authentic and life-giving play.

Vital ministries take grief seriously. As we allow ourselves and encourage others to experience grief, we do more for ourselves and our communities than we might think. We clear a space in our souls for the slow work of God that continually beckons us to new and sustaining life. Grief is the work that we do with the confident trust that God will, in fact, bring new life out of the physical or emotional ashes and rubble. Attending to emotions is hard work, but it also has incredible benefit for pastoral leadership. We meet God in our emotional lives, in the depth of pain and loss as well as in the elation and joy of play. These experiences are intimately related. Anyone who has tried to do something new in ministry without giving adequate attention to the emotions associated with loss eventually realizes the cost of this effort. Authentic and vital pastoral leadership embraces the hard work of grief and the experience of loss as well as the joy of play.[14]

The process of grief changes people and communities. Grief, when properly tended and cared for, has some of the qualities of play that opens us to new and unimagined possibilities. Grieving is a recurrent process for most people and communities. In the natural rhythm—the ebb and flow—of grief in life and ministry, we find space for the ability to play. Attention to the process of grief, though difficult, encourages the ability to play with a graceful and natural ease. Creatively playful pastoral leaders and communities, as ironic as it may seem, are willing to die over and over again to preconceived notions and to allow the brilliance and mystery of God to emerge in new ministries.

Pastoral leaders can suggest practical means for attending to grief. We may:

- Set aside time for reflection at a retreat house,
- schedule regular times to meet with a trusted friend,
- commit to a daily devotion that could include such practices as sitting in silence for a specified period each day and reading/ praying with the psalms,
- create a regular time in a daily calendar to pay attention and allow feelings to surface, whatever they may be.

Grief asks that we retreat from everyday life activities and accept the tears, which are a natural extension of these feelings. Through practice, we may learn to "let grief be"; we do not attempt to control, to mask, or to hide the feelings. Clearing a space for the grief, just as we might clear a space for play in our lives, may be the single most important commitment we can make.

Worship and other religious services help people connect with the process of grieving. For both individuals and communities, special services at holiday times and anniversary dates of deaths and other losses can be especially meaningful to those who are consciously grieving as well as those who may be less aware of any particular loss in their lives. When we "clear a space" to grieve, the process of grieving also clears a new space within us. The psalmist prays, "Create in me a clean heart, O God, and put a new and right spirit within me." (Psalm 51:10). Grieving, in the ancient words of this sacred prayer, cleanses the heart and renews the spirit. The process of grief has its own rhythms and dimensions and is best experienced in a non-controlling way. We cannot force grief any more than we can force genuine and authentic play. Both experiences, as surprising as it may sound, come as a gift.

The connection between grief and play is not an artificial one since both are movements of the soul. The absence of grieving in most public settings relates to repressed emotion and the absence of genuine play, of exhibiting a spirit of openness and flexibility to the options available to our most pressing problems and concerns. When our hearts are opened by the profound and life-altering dimension of grieving, we are also open to the soul-renewing aspect of responsible adulthood playfulness. This type of play is not intended or expected to provide an avoidance of personal or world problems.

Churches have traditionally been places where people can grieve within the context of worship and within a supportive community. Pastoral leaders stand on historically solid theological ground as we help people through the cathartic process of grief. Without "grieving space," the emotions of sadness, loss, and despair get locked inside and may manifest as bouts of depression, unexplained anger and frustration, hostility, and/or alienation from community.

Grieving for Many Kinds of Losses

When I served as a pastor of a small urban congregation and worked as a part-time chaplain at a large urban hospital, I experienced grief related to death and grief associated with other kinds of losses. I provided a pastoral presence at the bedside for dying people, their families, and friends. In this context, I could sense and observe the palpability of grief—the variety and intensity of emotions, and the love that gives rise to it all. As a pastor of a congregation in the context of a changing neighborhood with dwindling membership, I saw a different aspect of grieving. Parishioners struggled to understand themselves and their mission in light of changing circumstances. They needed help with moving through a grief process. Some people were mourning for the days when the pews were filled, when the Sunday school was brimming with children, when the church still owned the manse that had to be sold to pay off a minister who had sued the judicatory for wrongful termination. Immersion in these two different contexts of ministry taught me that grief has personal and communal dimensions.

Still, the challenges in finding space to grieve are often surprising. I once stood in the grocery store as a friend moved through the checkout line. As I waited minding my own business, a man walked by and said, "What's wrong? You look like you just lost your best friend!" I was left speechless. We are expected in our culture to put on a happy face when in reality we need to clear a space for grief for others and ourselves. Clearing a space for grief allows us to create a proper container for a powerful emotion, a place where grief may be nurtured and incubated so that we learn to live with that grief and beyond it.

Another minister tells a story from childhood.

> *One day she noticed her mother sitting at the kitchen table crying. The little girl moved toward her mother and asked, "Mommy, why are you crying?" The mother responded with: "I'm not crying." This*

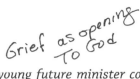
Grief as opening to God

young future minister concluded that crying must be a terrible, shameful thing since her mother needed to lie about it.

Many of us carry similar internal messages about grieving, and about the tears and emotions that accompany the process. We face a challenge in negotiating the space for private as well as public grieving. Since the expression of grief can leave us feeling emotionally vulnerable, it is important to establish protective barriers that can help guard the experience.

Personal and communal aspects of grieving unite in the image of Mary sitting at the empty tomb of Jesus and openly weeping (John 20:11). Mary expects to find Jesus, and weeps when she does not. Two angels redirect her attention to where the one who has died can be found.[15] Private grieving has become public and transformational. As the gospel passage makes evident, grieving has a theological dimension. Even as griefs shakes our bodies and finds expressesion in our tears, it transforms our experience and opens our perspective to God's holy presence in our lives.

Grieving is a process that attunes us to the emotional rhythm in our lives as pastoral leaders. Experiential knowledge of the grief process allows leaders to recognize and care for the grief of others through supportive leadership care practices. We'll consider several other connections between grief and pastoral ministry that help develop the capacity to trust, the foundation of playful creativity.

Pastoral leaders, especially those who minister to marginalized people and communities, must pay attention to the dynamic of shame.[16] The shame that comes with "not fitting"—a sense of being not good enough or defective in some way—can be powerful, and at times overwhelming, and can influence grief for individuals and communities. We find shame frequently in the ministry. Communities feel shame over not being able to attract new members in spite of all their efforts. Colorful fliers, community events, and welcoming words from members sometimes may fail to increase membership. Congregations unable to attract new members may feel shame and begin to question their worth. Standards set by expectation of growth are not met and the community may lose their sense of purpose and mission. Pastoral ministers can help guide communities through an experience of shame, first, by assisting people constructively to question the social and religious standards against which they may be measuring themselves, and second, to grieve the loss of attachment to those standards. Congregations can begin to set realistic expectations and evaluate progress against new standards.

A meaningful pastoral presence and response helps to heal the wound of shame and influences the ability for people grow in relationship with God and one another. Small churches and their members may be particularly vulnerable to the experience of shame. Consider the story of one such community.

> An electrical fire destroyed South Congregational Church, but grief and shame did not limit their future. Church membership had long been on the decline, and the destruction of the beloved building was one more burden on a struggling church. Grief over the loss of the building commingled with shame felt by the shrinking congregation. The pastor, sensitive to the process of grieving, did not press ahead too quickly with plans for a new building. Rather, time was devoted to experiencing grief for the old building with all the history and experiences that it symbolized. Finally, the pastor gathered members to meet with an architect for a new building. Design features of the old church — the pitched roof and mixture of stained and clear class — were incorporated into the new space. The small congregation now had a building to reflect its newer identity. The pastoral leader had met the congregational members in their pain and led them to imagine something new together. Their new identity acknowledged their history.

A number of significant pastoral issues relate to shame and grief for misfit persons and congregations. Working through these dynamics enables the possibility for playful purposefulness to re-emerge. Pastors and other congregational leaders can be helpful in several ways.

First, pastors can become more aware of the relationship between shame and grief. Shame reflects a sense of inferiority, or of being a flawed self or flawed community. The assumption is that there is inherently something wrong with us. Shame can overcome individuals and congregations by limiting action and imagination. Shame confines us to a limited sense of personhood and community; shame, in its negative and insidious forms, shrivels the soul and leads to harmful and destructive patterns of relationship. Attending to the process of grief helps ease constriction of shame and allows for sharing gifts in community.

Second, pastors can attend to the process of grief as a means to allow persons and congregations to open their hearts in empathic connection with one another. As loss, pain, and confusion subside, people and congregations tend to grow in awareness of the "non-negotiables," the core values and commitments that sustain our lives.[17] We may not arrive easily at knowledge of these convictions. The term "non-negotiables" may sound rigid and inflexible, even a contradiction to the experience of play itself. In soulful play and grief we become more deeply aware of what we value. One of my own non-negotiables is my need to have a period of silence everyday. The conditions and duration of this practice may vary but it provides space for the experience of both grief and joy. For congregations, non-negotiables are expressed in terms of core values and commitments; South Church—after the fire—recommitted to their ministry and mission in the community. An experience of loss and grief opened the congregation to a period of questioning, evaluating, and eventually re-committing to God and one another. In short, loss and grief eventually opened their emotional hearts to something that could be done. Attending to the pain gave the community access to a new way to play.

✗ The vitality of playful misfithood comes with knowing and claiming one's core values and commitments, one's non-negotiables, even when they are in tension with those of other people. Grief calls us to awareness of our own finitude, the limited nature of our lives. In light of this awareness, grief calls forth a regular inventory of our core commitments in order to refocus or reinvest in life-giving directions. We may discover that the non-negotiables have shifted as we enter a new phase in our ministries or personal lives.

Third, through grief work, pastors can encourage the growth of personal self-confidence and purposeful congregational mission. Self-confidence and congregational purpose combines a basic trust in self with the ability to interact with assurance in others.[18] In colloquial language, self-confidence is often described as "filling out our skin" or "blossoming into community." Self-confidence may grow in direct proportion to the ability to live in mutual relationship with others, capable of knowing one's own direction and also of being able to influence and be influenced by others. Self-confidence can be strengthened from the inside out, and confirmed from the outside in, each time an individual or community takes fruitful action to engage with the world and to learn from mistakes. This basic sense of life itself is what Winnicott calls "self-experience."[19] Grief helps to build confidence of the self and community by the encounter with what Paul Tillich calls the Ground of Being, the communion of God that exists beyond naming—in, beyond, beneath, throughout all experience.

People who have experienced any form of alienation or abuse may have trouble trusting their own "self-experience." They may withdraw into themselves, experience isolation and depression, and have difficulty developing and maintaining meaningful relationships. When for any reason the ability to trust is damaged, people may simultaneously experience a psychological as well as a religious and spiritual breakdown because, as Ann Ulanov writes, "self-experience gives us experience of God."[20] Connection to self-experience provides a sense of vitality; we have a sense of being "more alive" and in touch with authentic truth and deep wisdom. Abuse can separate us from ourselves and others as well as make us feel like we are separated from God. Pastoral leaders need to make informed referrals to trained experts such as pastoral counselors and nonpastoral professionals such as psychologists or therapists who can best help people who have been abused. In general, pastoral leaders who know themselves can be indispensable in helping others tap their own self-experience. Our self-experience is a source of primary creativity, that which makes us authentically who we are.[21]

Grieving and Playing toward Wholeness

Intentional grieving leaves us feeling depleted and exhausted, or as if dead on the inside. Yet through grief we become more aware of ourselves as fully alive. Connection with this vitality, our primary source of creativity, strengthens what Craig Dykstra calls an "internal gyroscope" for ministry.[22] We can trust that this internal gyroscope will help us move skillfully between the "in-balance" and "off-balance" rhythm of ministry. This state of nonequilibrium, which we all too often resist or fear, is the place that allows for systems and persons to change and grow.[23]

At a social gathering, someone approached me and commented on the luminaria I described in the opening of this chapter. "I noticed your school for the first time. There were all of these white bags lined up on the lawn. What were they for?" I sensed the impulse to explain my understanding of the symbolism of the candles and all the preparation and care that went into the actual experience. I couldn't adequately capture in words what it was like to be present for this meaningful day, so I simply stated, "We were remembering all the Saints who have gone before us." Play and grief, while difficult to capture in words, nevertheless ground us in the experience of life and ministry. In the midst of creative play as well as in soul-absorbing grief, we paradoxically recognize ourselves as deeply interconnected with God and one another.

The luminaria burned well into the night on All Saints Day. Lured by the flickering beauty of the lights, people paused to reflect and to contemplate; they entered the interior of the heart. Off-balance in these moments, we are touched by an experience much wider and more intimate than we can even name. We know ourselves, in the presence of awe-filled mystery, as off-balance and yet completely whole.

Questions for Personal and Group Reflection

1. What is your first remembrance of grief? Recall what triggered the process for you and what the experience was like. What messages did you receive from family and friends about the grief?

2. What patterns or rhythms of grief are recognized in your church or community? Are there any significant people or leaders who help with the process? What is their role?

3. Recall an image or phrase from Scripture that has sustained you or your community in times of grief and loss. How has God met you in that place?

4. After a transition in the congregation—loss of a significant member, moving to a new location, or change in pastoral leadership—how were members helped to grieve the loss and encouraged to celebrate and play into a new beginning? If this didn't happen, what has been the spiritual and psychological cost to the members and the community?

5. What contributes to renewal in your life or in your community? Has an experience of "letting go" enabled the experience of play or a new-found joy?

6. How does fear and resistance interrupt the grief process for you or your community?

7. How have movements of playful creativity lightened your load and allowed for moving forward?

8. Identify practices in your personal and community's life that have helped renew trust and contribute to healing.

9. What experiences of shame have influenced your community? Have there been transformational moments or glimpses of God's call throughout? How so?

10. Describe your level of comfort with emotions. How is space created in your personal and congregational life for tears of grief?

How can we play with/in our grief?

3 Plays and Playing
Discovering Authentic Selfhood

> This holy play requires discipline, and a long memory. This holy play
> asks of us vulnerability to grace and to one another. This holy
> play invites us to a profound trust that God has created us to delight
> in the gift of life.
>
> —Don E. Saliers
> *Worship Comes to Its Senses*

*Elinor Fuchs, professor of drama at Yale, might never have imagined
that the relationship with her mother would take the turn it did.
Diagnosed with Alzheimer's disease, her mother in the last years
of her life had diminished capacity for interaction. Fuchs used her
"theatrical imagination" to help her cope with a situation that might
otherwise have been quite grim. She engaged in improvisational
conversation with her mother, taking as reality whatever her mother
"believed at the moment."[1]*

Fuchs responded creatively and humorously to her mother who also
enjoyed a good laugh. Through Fuchs' creative play, a bond of care
and love deepened in the relationship with her mother that brought
meaning and sense that otherwise might not have been possible.

We practice with theatrical plays because we "set the stage," as it
were, for re-rehearsing already established relationships and preparing
for the not-yet-even-imagined encounters in our lives. Like Fuchs
who fostered a deep relationship with her own mother through the
experience of Alzheimer's Disease, we, too, may be surprised at what
can be called forth from within our souls when the situation warrants.

By practicing with theatrical plays, we achieve voice and strength in living our own scripts as people of God, and respond with newfound creativity and open hearts to our loved ones and neighbors alike.[2]

Transformative Conversations: Healing Power of Plays for Ministry

The enactment of play scripts is healing for individuals and communities. From my experience as a pastor and theological educator, I know that talking about theology and doctrine can all too easily become overly rational and disembodied from the everyday lives of most Christians. I often sense that there is more energy in a room than we are able to harness. So I use skits, role plays, and enactments with biblical characters to help people get in touch with the many aspects of stories. In one experimental course, entitled "Play Theory and Plays: Creativity in Pastoral Ministry," I collaborated with a colleague who teaches drama. Much to my delight, students preparing for various types of pastoral leadership—parish ministry, campus chaplaincy, hospice care, and retreat ministry—enrolled. In our course as well as in ministry, the real work is often to pay attention to frequently overlooked gestures, movements, or fleeting moments of feeling and insight. As one participant commented, "I learned so much in this course, and it's also very practical even though I can't always explain exactly what *that* is." While difficult to capture in words, the aesthetic enriches the practices of ministry. Theatrical play frees people to explore new creative possibilities for life with God, and lays the groundwork for meaningful theological reflection and growth of relationship in community.

> *Theatrical play frees people to explore new creative possibilities for life with God, and lays the groundwork for meaningful theological reflection and growth of relationship in community.*

The capacity for play is within us.[3] Play and plays give us insight into the intricate nature of human relationships and relationships with God. In playing, we challenge myths such as the possibility for perfection.[4] Faithful living has many complexities and contradictions, and theatrical plays serve as a touchstone for theological conversation, which can surface issues of value, significance, meaning, and as well as theological themes of forgiveness, redemption, and salvation. We don't sit in judgment on the play as audience members, but get ourselves up on the stage as its actors, learning what it's like from the inside out to become and interact *as that character*. Reading and enacting plays is a full-bodied way of doing theology that is deeply playful, which integrates our intellects and emotions. Play therefore is not just about having fun. Sensitive and painful personal and social issues emerge. This chapter considers the indirect, nonlinear insights that play fosters in the practice of ministry. We cultivate an aesthetic sensibility, an appreciation for art and beauty. We also grow into authentic selfhood and community as the beloved creatures of God. With play readings and enactments we contextualize a way of playing in congregations.

A Way of Practicing Theology

A minister colleague and her husband are one of three couples who gather with their spouses for a play reading about six times a year. The group of six includes three Presbyterian ministers and one United Church of Christ minister along with a psychologist and an engineer. The idea of forming such a group was generated by a Presbyterian minister whose parents were part of a play-reading group a generation ago.

The basic "structure" for the evening is a shared meal that rotates among the homes of different members. After dinner, the group reads a play with preferably not more than six characters. Group members, aside from perhaps the person who has chosen the play, will not have usually read the script in advance.

People choose the character whose part they will read, careful not to skip ahead in the script. Group members engage in a spontaneous reading of the text, and are often surprised by how much they like or dislike a particular character. They discover hidden or submerged aspects of their own personalities that awaken with the reading of a particular character's lines.

Play of this nature allows people to enter the worldview of the play and to assume the character's persona. Participants discover a capacity within them for reading a part they may not have chosen in advance. At times, participants experience deep satisfaction in playing a part because of close identification with the character. One highly capable minister who strives for intellectual and emotional balance in her life and ministry enjoyed assuming the role of a neurotic psychologist. Participants sometimes anticipate they will like a particular character only to discover otherwise. Others in the group know one another well enough to realize why their companions like to play certain parts.

This practice offers a number of benefits. Enacting plays gives people permission to engage spontaneously, and in an imaginative way to assume new identities. In the words of one participant, the "spontaneous sphere" is that realm where we don't actually know what's going to happen. We have to stay open without any preconceived notions of how it will unfold until the conclusion of the play. Whereas a skilled actor would work out the scenes and staging in advance, these participants enact their parts as they observe an ongoing revelation. People get to be participant-observers: to watch as they also participate in the play, and to observe how relationships develop among other characters in the play. Participants learn to trust the wisdom of the process and the playwright who constructed the play.

Opening the Heart of the Play Themes

Playing with plays opens the individual heart and the heart of the community in a number of ways. As the above illustration indicates and experience in the seminary classroom confirms, valuable theological and psychological activities and insights emerge in playing with plays. Play reading and enactments:

1. provide an intentional gathering of community for play.
2. give an opportunity for inter-religious or interfaith interaction. This is a nonthreatening way of exploring themes and topics. As significant religious or faith matters emerge, people can discuss the issues as they relate to characters in the play.
3. allow us to discover aspects of ourselves, develop relationships with others in community, and grow into the fullness of the *imago Dei,* the image of God. We might even come to appreciate how much we value what we originally disliked in a character. We can develop awareness about different ways of being and relating through plays.
4. show conflict, an inevitable aspect of living, and it's many layers: conflict internal to each person, conflict that emerges on an interpersonal level, and social conflict that involves large groups of people pitted against one another. Enacting play scripts can show people constructive as well as destructive ways of living with conflict.
5. help us get to the heart of difficult issues, including forgiveness, torn relationships, illness, death, and unexpected alliances.
6. help us to become participant-observers. People may be able to glimpse or experience something new about themselves, others, and God without having it explained to them. On a basic level, we get to watch even as we participate in a process. This movement between active participation and rest allows the mind to make connections and associations on its own. With this practice, the Holy Spirit finds room in our hearts to beckon us toward something imaginative and new.
7. let participants strengthen their own sense of "voice." Additionally, creative improvisation, based on knowledge of the characters, urges us to step off into the unknown. This may be initially frightening because we are often concerned about the performance aspect of the playing. We fear the judgment of others, making fools of ourselves, or making mistakes. If we recognize the fear in ourselves and others without denying or diminishing it, this process can be *character-building.*

Reading and enacting plays gives practice at encountering a different worldview. We gradually learn to navigate through unfamiliar territory, perhaps with a growing sense of curiosity. The pastoral ministry of listening can be like this, whether we serve as pastors or community lay leaders. Listening to the *story* of another person with its conflicts, tensions, struggles, hopes, and joys is, in some sense, to encounter a *script* with its attendant expression of language and feelings that may or may not be familiar. Authentic listening, and a willful ability to engage in meaningful and faithful conversation with the other person, asks that we engage with respectful curiosity to their story. Mindful of our own life story, we listen to the story of the other person *as if* it were our own. This is what it means to *practice empathy*.

A Means of Talking in Character and Talking about Character

Enactment of a play puts us in touch with a fuller dimension of what it's like to inhabit another person's world. Instead of talking about a character from a distance, we learn what it's like to *become* a character. In developing the subtext, we imagine the character's thoughts, perspectives, and feelings. We experience the tenor of relationships between and among characters in the play. Most of us, however, are not readily able to enact a character; it may take time for some people to become comfortable with the idea. What follows is a framework to help pastoral leaders interpret people's comfort with plays and playing.

- Safe Zone: Reading a play and having a discussion about it is one way to engage the literature; this level of engagement, intellectually engaged but relatively uninvolved emotionally is safe for most of us. This practice allows us to get to know the characters and the themes in the play. Talking about characters is less risky because it doesn't ask us necessarily to reveal anything about ourselves, even though we indirectly reveal our own thoughts, feelings, responses, and social location as we reflect about the characters. This is a safe zone for most people because we talk about the material in an intellectual and often abstract way. We don't necessarily risk anything of ourselves at this level of the process.

- Risk Zone 1: Enacting the characters of a play through a staged reading, whether standing or moving around, is a different kind of experience than simply reading a description about the play or reading the play by ourselves. Such enactment asks that people

movement

engage their entire bodies, not just their heads. It feels a bit more risky and vulnerable to stand or to move around a room than it does to sit and read the play aloud.

- Risk Zone 2: Creative improvisation builds on knowledge of a character and extends it. While much more imaginative, improvisation is also much riskier because it asks people creatively to engage one another with their own words and gestures based on what they already know about a character. Participants bring their own personalities to the enactment of a character, revealing something about themselves as well as the character through this imaginative exercise. People may experience inhibitions, feeling self-conscious about their abilities or fearful of performing. We can exercise sensitivity to people's hesitations and inhibitions by encouraging them to practice this improvisation in pairs or small groups. Entering the worldview of a character and speaking in the voice and actions of a characters gets us "inside the skin" of another. Participants get in touch with feelings and ideas of what it is actually like to be that person. Such enactments can produce a sense of exhilaration, dread, fear, or joy. Getting inside the character can be an edifying form of experiential learning as we come to know more about ourselves as well as the characters.

- Interplay Between Zones: The "trust zone" or "interplay zone" is when we move back and forth from talking *about* the characters to talking *in* character. After we talk about the character, enact the character through staged readings, and even creatively improvise as if we were the character, we can return to talking about the character with new awareness. The interplay zone is moving back and forth from talking about characters to interacting as if one were the character back again to conversation about the interaction. The purpose is to engage in both action and reflection. I call this the trust zone because a sense of community cohesion emerges when we enact the play, improvise based on knowledge of the play, as well as reflect on the themes and issues that the play raises for us as leaders and people of faith. The trust zone is

Great Idea for interplay this Do in class ★★

the area that can alternatively feel safe and risky for people: we generally feel vulnerable as we act and improvise and more confident when we talk. Creating a space for various kinds of interaction around the themes of a play permits people to take emotional and intellectual leaps, and in so doing, build confidence within themselves and connection in community.

The Entire Cast of Characters Within

Enacting plays is one way for people in religious communities to get in touch with, from a nonjudgmental perspective, the many characters that inhabit our interior world. We all reckon with voices inside our heads; these voices are the characters that, metaphorically speaking, reside within us, including the critic, the pleaser, the rebel, the nurturer, the self-centered one, the judge, the bargainer.[5] Each of these voices represents a character that plays either a leading or supporting role in our internal play script. Understanding the values, demands, wants, and desires of each of these internal characters enlarges our ability to relate with characters such as these in real life as well as characters and leaders in the biblical story.[6] So, for example, if we are accustomed to ignoring or silencing the critic within us because we cannot bear to listen to it, we are more likely to ignore or silence people who we view as critics. A play script can act as a reflective mirror of those internal characters and voices. Learning to differentiate between the characters and to appreciate the relationships between them increases our self-awareness and enhances our relationships with others.

Enacting plays provides a catharsis or an emotional release because as we participate in this artistic expression, we borrow the language of another to express what is, in some sense, our own. We identify with the character(s). The world of the play becomes our world as our attention becomes more drawn into the life of the characters and what matters to them. The play and its characters resonate within us even after the play has concluded. Themes and phrases linger with us. It is important to pay attention to the language and themes that *linger and resonate* because they, too, reflect something about us.

Listening and Sharing the Themes That Echo

Designated leaders can invite participants to share particular lines or themes that resonate for them within the play. Participants may also want to express what these lines capture for them, such as an insight about God, or a perplexing aspect of human relationships. A nuanced turn of phrase in play reading and enactments can evoke deep meanings and reflection for participants. Each person will have a different reading of the play based on personal experience and viewpoint. An exercise in sharing meanings is not intended to create a unified reading of the play, but to share the various phrases and lines that resonate and echo for people. A discussion of what makes the line personally meaningful or provocative can be valuable as long as it does not become an exercise to convince others of what is most important about the play. Giving voice to that which echoes within our minds strengthens theological honesty and integrity in our church communities.

Play enactments can be healing because we feel less isolated and alone in the world. We are more connected to ourselves and one another through this process. The practice of playing and play reading enlarges our worldview and lures us toward integration and wholeness.

An experience with play and play scripts quickly reveals something: we have entered a whole new world and at the same time we haven't. We hover between reality and non-reality. In this transitional space between our own experience and the world of the play, creative impulses emerge.

Getting into Character as a Way to Experience the True Self

Some people may dismiss the practice of playing with plays as an exercise in frivolity, delegating it to the realm of fantasy. This unfortunate assumption views imaginative exercise as having no contact with the so-called real world. Imaginative experience, far from being narrow, though, can actually enlarge our sense of community and make us more aware of the Holy Spirit's movement, drawing us inward to know the true self and outward to express this self in the world. While closely connected in meaning, imagination and fantasy share one distinguishing feature that is helpful for playing and enacting play scripts: imagination emerges from the creative linking between the "seen" and "unseen" world of images and symbols, whereas fantasy draws energy from an existence independent of lived reality.[7] Play itself and theatrical play reading is valuable in ministry in so far as it helps bridge us toward the real world where our faith is put to the test and where good ministry bears fruit. Instead of pulling us away from the real world into fantasy, playing may stimulate creative actions we might genuinely take in our communities to respond to the effects of such serious matters as war, poverty, abuse, illness, and conflict.

Pastoral ministry calls forth from us the ability to oscillate from pain and sorrow to joy and exhilaration. Within the span of a day or week, we might meet with a couple preparing for marriage and care for grieving family members at a memorial service. Being able to move responsively and genuinely from one experience to another is a form of pastoral play, being ready and able to enter into a lived situation and interact contextually and appropriately. The experience of the other remains distinct from our own, yet we are simultaneously connected with it. Pastoral leaders can help to foster playful Christian people and communities as they recognize, affirm, and draw out budding creativity, rather than squelching insights and ideas that may initially seem different.

Giving Expression and Voice to the Voiceless

An example of developing a community play illustrates how to give voice to the experience of those who are often voiceless. A minister trained in educational theater works cooperatively with communities of women to foster self and communal empowerment. The first task is to gather as much information as possible through interviews with women who have experienced a particular historical event or are most familiar with a particular topic. Then the educational theater troupe—

"gently and lovingly" in the minister's words — tries various combinations of words, movements, images, characters and storyline in order to capture the most authentic and meaningful way to reflect in dramatic form the lives of the people they have interviewed. The purpose is to share the history of a people including their struggles and celebrations as an alternative and empowering means to imagine and live into a new future.[8]

One specific project funded by the women's division of the Presbyterian Church (U.S.A.) creates a partnership between women of the Presbyterian Church in Guatemala and women's church groups in the United States. The church in Guatemala has traditionally been quite patriarchal and oppressive to the faith experience of women. This project seeks to build the confidence of women and express their unique stories and struggles of faith. The eventual goal is the creation of a bilingual play that promotes mutual education and faithful solidarity. Leaders will help the women with community building, story sharing and collecting, and theater skill building and collaborative playwriting. The women's groups may choose to share their developing insights through a short play, series of scenes, a written document, multidisciplinary arts presentation, or simply enjoying the processes of creation.

Community play practice is a way of living theology by telling faith stories and struggles that are meaningful for us and hearing the responses from other Christian communities. This is one creative and communal experience of play that opens the hearts and lives of women even as the practice challenges patriarchal assumptions and values in the church. This play becomes a powerful form of prayer as people give voice to God the yearnings of their hearts and souls.

Mending the Internal Split

Play is in part about healing the division inside, an internal mending between the true and false selves, the face we show the world and the self who lives within.[9] Our genuine selves include both aspects of who we are. It's not that one self is good and one self is bad, even though we may sometimes think of it this way. We have many reasons for protecting the tender, vulnerable inner self, many times to prevent personal or social suffering or wounding. Authentic selfhood in God is about not denying or disregarding aspects of ourselves, but embracing our full selves just as God does. With a sense of fearless play, we may come to recognize and integrate those disowned and perhaps disregarded aspects into a vital whole.

With a sense of fearless play, we may come to recognize and integrate those disowned and perhaps disregarded aspects of ourselves into a vital whole.

Play is one means of entering the mystery of life and ministry. Play opens us to the spirit of discovery or being more open to not knowing. A temporary suspension of knowing can lead us down paths that are authentic. Such is the lesson that Elinor Fuchs gleaned from the improvised dialogues with her mother in the advanced stages of Alzheimer's disease. Her mother's heart was made glad by the encounter, even if the conversation was nonsensical.

In a ministry of play, we allow ourselves to discover ourselves and others in a new and unencumbered way. We set aside our biases and assumptions and allow the experience to teach us what we need to know in order to respond to another person. Releasing ourselves to experience the moment allows for the possibility of meeting face to face with another's True Self. The authentic and true self cannot be manufactured or contrived; it is rather glimpsed and experienced in sometimes fleeting as well as sustained moments. Playing with plays can be a valuable form of teaching in itself; people learn by engaging rather than by being "talked at" or having things "explained" to them. Pastoral leaders are instrumental and effective in ministry when we create contexts and situations in which people can experience this type of learning.

nonverbal play as well / Bodies don't lie

Creating a Good-Enough Environment for Play

The play of ministry best occurs within set boundaries. Pastors need to create a safe environment so that a vulnerable, wounded person can begin to feel trust and move to a new relationship with God and other participants. Play is partly about creating a safe, secure, trustworthy environment that gives people permission to experiment with new ideas and patterns of faithful living.

Let's consider some important elements that help make an environment safe for creative play and improvisation.

> *Continuity* of the environment which assists in the development of personality; *reliability* which makes the actions of caregivers predictable; *graduated adaptation* to the continually evolving needs of the child [person]; and *beholding* the *creative impulse*" [emphasis is Winnicott's].[10]

These qualities can serve to develop the "good-enough" context in which pastoral ministers, like "power-assisted steering on a motorbus,"[11] cultivate thoughtful, lively, and creative ministries. In creating a good enough environment, we draw on the strengths already present in the community and set the tone for further development. Eventually, people may learn to give themselves permission to grasp new learning opportunities that they previously considered unimaginable.

Use of Drama Skills Calls Forth a Metaphor for Ministry: Pastor as Play Director

This certainly is a misfit image. The pastor is not the only one who can be the director; appointed lay people can do this as well. With informal group gatherings, someone could be selected as play director, and serve in the capacity of what we ordinarily might call a facilitator. So the analogy is really with how we engage this type of small group ministry in the church. It can be a complement to other groups or one aspect of what already established groups do together.

Directing principles also serve as useful guideposts to help people of faith deepen authentic relationships. These process skills help us learn about our authentic selves as we practice play.[12] Leaders can use the directing principles in one of two ways: as an implicit checklist for monitoring and balancing group dynamics, or as an explicit guideline for focusing the attention and accountability of all members.

I have adopted terms developed by my colleague Fredericka Berger for her Chancel Drama lectures to describe the technical process of rehearsing and shaping a play and redefined them to describe various aspects of the ministry of play.[13] I sense that every pastoral leadership and care interaction has a theological rationale, whether or not we are actually aware of it in any particular situation. What we say and do sends a message. What we enable others to say and do also sends a message. Let's see how these drama terms can help guide effective ministry.

Audibility: Everyone needs to be heard; can we make sense of what another is saying? When an audience is present, they need to be able to hear clearly what everyone is saying. Those who speak softly must practice talking more loudly when engaged in play. The ability to he heard by others, and to hear ourselves as well, is also an important aspect of spiritual life. To speak and be heard means that others must reckon with us; we are a character in the play and in their lives. Questions to consider are the following:

- How can I keep my voice strong?
- What contributes to weakness of voice?

Visibility: A director is concerned with staging a play so that everyone in the audience can see, but we can also reflect on visibility metaphorically. What keeps us from seeing others: Our own preoccupations? Thoughts? Concerns for how we will be seen? Being seen, by others and also by God, is a primary human need. In our play practices in the church, we make sure that everyone is seen as we need to be seen, as people of faith and as actors in a play, regardless of the role's importance. Everyone needs to see and to be seen.

- How do we demonstrate that we have seen someone?
- How does another imagine he or she is seen?

Emphasis: In drama there are two complementary aspects to emphasis: visual and psychological. Visual emphasis, in the sense of how and where actors are placed on age, should reflect the character's psychological state. Psychological emphasis can be captured by gesture and tone of interaction among the actors within the play. Visual emphasis also allows a director to highlight the importance of a character through prominent placement on the stage. A director creatively adapts visual emphasis to highlight and capture the psychological state of the actors. As play participants, we notice themes and language that deserve emphasis and then share this with others. We pay attention to the emphasis that others give to particular scene, relationship, or language in the play as a way to notice what draws attention. Engaging in this practice, by analogy, helps us to listen more closely to the stories we tell in our daily lives and how we tell those stories in our own lives. We can ask:

- What gets emphasized?
- What seems to be left out?

We emphasize for many reasons: a subject is particularly captivating or problematic or through a desire to draw attention to ourselves or a commitment to an ideology. Emphasis can be communicated through gestures, body movement, language intensity or inflection.

Variety: This includes doing things differently to keep the audience awake. In ministry variety helps to draw people's attention but is not the same thing as entertainment. Variety is introduced to capture people's imagination in as many ways as possible to draw us closer to the heart of God. In a play, the actors interact in a variety of ways: shifting the standing places; speaking with changes in voice inflection; drawing from a reservoir, rather than just one stream, of emotions. A drama director must pay attention to variety in order to interpret the play meaningfully and to engage the audience. Variety produces different ways of experiencing and seeing. In play reading and enactments in local communities, taking turns with characters' parts can be one way to infuse the experience with variety. Variety is meant to enhance the experience of the play, not make it confusing or crowded. So, too, can the principle of variety be beneficial for ordering our personal and communal lives of faith. Variety in ways of praying, worshipping, working for peace with justice—provided it does not intentionally overwhelm or confuse people—can nurture growth and faith in the love of God and neighbor. Playing with plays is one such way to develop this practice.

- How could I add variety to a comfortable routine?
- Where could variety enliven something that has become monotonous?

Focus: Focus also has a couple of significant elements: the director controls the focus of the audience by staging a play in a certain manner. Focus also refers to the actor's skilled ability to inhabit a character. One aspect of focus relates to someone taking control to direct the attention of a group; the other aspect relates to an internal ability of an actor to block out external distractions. Focus, whether it comes with assistance from another person or from within our psychological resources, harnesses the energy of attention so that we do not miss a pivotal experience. Through the skill of focusing attention within the context of reading or enacting a dramatic play, we pay attention to what captures or provokes us in the experience within us or between other characters.

- Where do I want to direct my focus?
- What turns my focus from where I intend it?

Pace: This is the rate of timing within the play as a whole, and includes the speed with which characters deliver their lines and the rhythm of interactions between the characters. Pace involves dramatic or creative tension and timing, and can affect how the audience engages the play.

When we attune ourselves to the natural rhythm of playing with plays, we can also move this awareness and skill into other dimensions of ministry. In church meetings, we may practice slowing down and breathing deeply, a body awareness exercise that gets people in touch with the Holy Spirit moving within. The purpose in this slowing down is not to make all of our meetings slow. Rather, as we become more aware of the natural rhythm of our own breathing, we awaken to the natural flow and rhythm of what actually needs to happen in a particular gathering. What is needed might even be a passionate and fast-paced discussion about a topic of importance to the community. Paying attention to the pace of our pastoral conversations gives information about the state of people's souls. Pastoral attention to the pace of conversational play can give us beginning clues to people's internal states: rapid-fire interactions can mean that people are busy, agitated, angry, stressed-out, or even excited, and enthusiastic; slower pacing may indicate thoughtfulness, a higher degree of introspection, or maybe even melancholy and depression. Pace gives information about the rhythm of our personal and community soul.

People of faith are often susceptible to the danger that keeps most people out of the natural rhythm, an all too prevalent busyness or tendency toward crowded living. God's rhythm is already present within creation. God's rhythm is present in our lives. Our job is to catch that rhythm and play on. Playing with plays helps communities cultivate an appreciation for this underlying rhythm.

• What can I do to be more aware of God's pace?

• In what situations would a change of pace be effective?

The imaginative and creative venture of playing with plays can be immensely beneficial for people of faith and the ministry of the church. Through script as well as improvisation we discover the capacity of language and gesture for creating bonds of healing within the human family. Pastoral ministry can be used to transform an intellectual exercise into an experience that opens our hearts and minds in surprising and stimulating ways.

Questions for Personal and Group Reflection

1. What assumptions or experiences either attract or scare you about play? If you could imagine any role for yourself, what would it be? What is your authentic role? Are you living that role now? What do you imagine it would be like to not play that role?

2. Choose two biblical characters from anywhere in the Bible, preferably from different books or even different testaments. Develop a brief dialogue between these two characters. What would you imagine them saying to each other about God from what you know about their life experiences?

3. Select a play — such as *Murder in the Cathedral* — to read with a group. Each participant should read the play in advance of a set group meeting. When reading the play, take turns reading various characters' parts so that no one person reads one character throughout the whole play. Afterward, discuss the experience with the group.

4. Using the typology outlined earlier (safe zone, risk zone, and interplay between zones), name specific practices that could guide your community in discussing and engaging in sensitive or controversial issues.

5. Imagine that different people in your community are cast members in a play. Who are the central players? Who are support people? Who are the behind the scenes people? Reflect on the relationships between and among the people. Is there room for creative improvisation or is everything already scripted?

6. Reflect on ways that reading or enacting play scripts can be transformational for facilitating interaction among people of different generations in your congregation, and for engaging the congregation with the wider community.

7. Of the drama skills identified, identify your strength and your growing edge. Which one do you most value? Least value?

8. People say, "That was 'out of character' for him/her." Consider a scenario in your life or in ministry when your authentic self was expressed when you were "out" of character. What was this like?

9. How have different characters/people revealed the face of God to you?

10. Where are you usually more comfortable—acting in the play or sitting in observation? Can you imagine shifting perspectives? What might be different?

4 Playful Teaching and Learning

For successful education there must always be a certain
freshness . . . Knowledge does not keep any better than fish.

— Alfred North Whitehead
The Aims of Education and Other Essays

The new pastor was invited to lunch by prominent members of the
congregation. Over a delicious meal with homemade pie for dessert,
a traditional Sunday lunch at a parishioner's home in this small
parish, they shared stories. They talked about people and families
in the church and how the community had changed over the years,
the folks who had moved away, those who didn't come to church any
more, and about the days when the pews overflowed with people.
Pastor John was learning more about the church that he was just
called to serve. Elder Tom and Deacon Helen also offered the new
pastor a pointed lesson in dynamics of this particular congrega-
tion. Elder Tom shared the story of when a new pastor had come
to the congregation a decade earlier and initiated a new policy for
training teachers. "He said that we needed to educate the teachers.
Well, that didn't go over so well," Elder Tom chuckled. "The next
Sunday all the teachers quit. They didn't need someone to tell them
how to teach! He learned real quickly."

Play has theological significance for teaching and learning in the
congregation. Pastors need to be as sensitive to *how* programs are
initiated as well as what is initiated. Play fosters a spirit of common
vision and commitment that allows pastors and congregations to

come together in their mutual ministries. Together we develop greater trust in God, ourselves, and our churches. Creative play engages heart and mind in teaching and learning for serendipitous and enthusiastic response to God.

Variations on Elder Tom's story are replicated in other congregations. Pastoral leaders, well-intentioned and focused in their ministries, forge ahead with plans without due consideration to the process as well as the content of communication. Lessons for pastors and others emerge from a pastoral theology of play.

- First, an educational theology of play privileges the more insignificant aspects of life as much as those deemed significant. Play delights in the mundane, and sparks enchantment with even the most ordinary of events.

- Second, a relational theology of play values the many dimensions of human relationship, including those that might be considered "merely social." A theology of play envisions that the emotional, psychological, and intellectual stimulation that comes from such interactions can deeply inform the meaning of our lives and ministries.

- Third, a theology of play recognizes the benefit of making way for, and embracing, wholehearted joy for its own sake as well as for the healing it can bring to our hearts.[1] This theology affirms that a joy-filled life is the birthright of all persons and communities.

- Finally, a relational theology of play takes into account personal, social, and institutional barriers as well as fractured relationships that can restrict the expression of creativity. A theology of play therefore is not naively optimistic in its analysis of personal and social relationships of power.[2]

Theological Insights for Educational Practice

Education needs to be seen in the congregation as an honorable and valuable aspect of our life together. The value and importance of the teaching role cannot be overemphasized, especially when pastors face a multitude of demands, including administration, pastoral care, evangelism programs, and stewardship campaigns. Pastoral leaders are also teachers, and practices associated with teaching can enhance the joy, exhilaration, discovery, and excitement of faith. Pastoral leaders must celebrate and reclaim the role of teacher as part of their pastoral identity.

Playful education is neither teacher focused nor specifically content focused, but primarily person focused in its approach. Playful education emphasizes:

- intrapersonal capacities: growth in self-awareness;
- interpersonal capacities: establishing and maintaining relationships within a group; and
- environmental sensitivity: paying attention to space and context.

Playful education is person focused and, yet, not individualistic in its approach to faith. Playful pastors remain committed to rigorous intellectual pursuits, and they are particularly aware of methods and practices that teach faith experientially. Play makes room for tackling difficult issues and entertaining pressing questions. But the participants themselves, and not the pastoral teacher alone, participate in negotiating these issues and questions. This does not mean, however, that the pastoral teacher has no agenda or focus for teaching. The pastoral teacher prepares an outline, a theme for the day, or a topic for discussion in addition to some reflection and reading relevant literature.

Playful pastoral educators, though, hold their agendas lightly, realizing that what people need to learn may be different from what they need to teach. Playful education thus starts from an attitude of not-knowing—a profound and deeply spiritual place—in which the pastoral teacher recognizes that God's Spirit is the primary teacher. Playful teachers know when to step out of the way so that their own needs to be in charge or viewed as knowledgeable become secondary to the teaching of the Holy Spirit. This can be a somewhat challenging place to stand initially but gives way to a more profound trust in God. Playful education practices are open-ended and allow God to call us to a new future in faith as individuals and communities. Are we available for this adventure?

Playful pastoral educators, though, hold their agendas lightly, realizing that what people need to learn may be different from what they need to teach . . . Playful teachers know when to step out of the way so that their own needs to be in charge or viewed as knowledgeable become secondary to the teaching of the Holy Spirit.

The person leading the story time asked the children gathered what they liked most about coming to church. One little girl announced happily that she enjoyed coming to church because it was a place to play.

Later, a group of adults reported on their most recent experience at a jurisdictional meeting of the church. Linking her report with what the child had said, one woman declared that play was, indeed, a meaningful part of her experience at the meeting where she learned a dance move that she proceeded to teach the congregation. Folks in the congregation awkwardly mimicked the movements as the person in front directed. Is this what the little girl meant by play?

Playful experience for adults is not simply about teaching dance moves, as positively intentioned as this was. Through play, our entire life of faith in God is imagined as creatively playful response to God's abundant love. By calling forth the creative spirit of God within and between each person and community, education frees people for exploration and encourages curiosity. As children playing the familiar game of hide-and-seek we used to say "olly, olly, ox-in-free" to call in those still hiding. Many will remember the exhilaration that comes from being able to run free after the period of hiding. We went screaming and yelling our way to the home-free zone. It was great. But as we grow older we lose our capacity to run free. We become more bound to adulthood, less free. Through play we can reclaim some of that child-hood freedom and use it to rediscover the deep joy of learning and re-connect more deeply with our faith. Play, then, is not meant to be games we implement during worship but as a way to approach learning that is deeply grounded in our faith. And the purpose of this learning is to free us to do the work of ministry, whether we are lay or ordained.

Some might expect that play makes us more self-centered in that we are caught up in what feels good for us. In reality, play as embodied theology, takes as its center the life of God in Christ. It respects and honors the other; it carries deep concern for the well-being of neighbor and creation, and it enlarges the circle of the church. I like to think that the Holy One smiles at such delightful ways of being in which adults as well as children in the faith community take play seriously.

Playful Education in the Church

Playful practices for educational ministries in the church do not require that everyone hold the same theological viewpoint or perspective. Such practices will thrive in communities that value diversity of opinion and perspective, those that do not require that everyone rigidly con-form to one model of living the Christian faith. If the purpose of edu-cation in the church is to nurture every unique person into the fullness of their stature in God, then we don't all have to fit one mold. We are free to become the creatively (mis)fit people God is calling us to be-come. People are free to respond to God's invitation toward shalom, a vision and reality in which all are welcome. Healthy and effective reli-gious misfits are people who, while responding to God's creative call in their lives, are also ethically engaged in learning in community with others.

Play Makes Space for Mistakes

One Sunday in worship I inadvertently finished reciting the Apostles' Creed ahead of my congregation because I had forgotten one entire line. After the service, a couple of prominent members greeted me warmly and commented about how *glad* they were to realize the minister makes mistakes. Still somewhat self-conscious, I realized in that moment that the blunder served an unintended purpose: it strengthened the bond of emotional intimacy between us by revealing my humanity. The members unconsciously felt that my mistake gave them permission to make mistakes themselves. Somehow, by the grace of the Holy Spirit, my error became a teachable moment in which we all learned that we need not be overly self-conscious about making mistakes.

In later worship leadership moments, especially while reciting creeds and prayers, I remembered this misstep. Play, in this case, allowed me to stay open and flexible for God's freeing activity. Making mistakes can be a potentially stifling experience if we become overly fearful of it happening again. Paradoxically, the more fearful and self-conscious we become, the greater the likelihood it *will* happen again. By responding playfully to the memory of my mistake, I was able to be forgiving of my own errors and claim humility and grace for my humanness.

Playful ministers make creative use of their mistakes. We show others that it is fine to make mistakes by allowing ourselves to fall down, metaphorically speaking. If we feel upset over our mistakes, this emotion is communicated to those around us. However, an attitude of what James Dittes calls *gracious nonchalance*[3] communicates something altogether different. By feeling free to make and acknowledge mistakes, we extend that freedom to others. However, in the case of egregious boundary crossings, great harm can be inflicted on others. Such errors in behavior and judgment are not the mistakes to which I refer. As well, intentional mistakes for the purpose of manipulation are not the point of this aspect of play. Theological play does not involve any intention of harm to participants and should be carefully monitored for such.

Mistakes reveal information and suggest that there is more to a story. Sigmund Freud noted that "slips of tongue" evidenced the conflicts within us.[4] We may say one thing and mean another. Attention to the mistakes we and others make may give clues as to actual thoughts or emotions.

*service of intentional mistake(s)   "Gracious Nonchalance"

Backwards- drop things mix up

Pastoral leaders with such attention may learn how people feel about themselves. Mistakes may indicate discomfort with a situation that a creative pastoral leader could assuage. Mistakes may also indicate stress, and an attentive pastor may discover difficulties related to work or family that will benefit from pastoral care and concern or from other professional attention.

Play as Faithfully Transgressing[5]

Play can be a faithful way to transgress and subvert assumed boundaries in religious practice because it generates enthusiasm and excitement and fosters bonds of love. Since the potential exists for the misuse of this practice, I emphasize that its engagement relies on the sound ethical judgment of leaders and lay people alike.

Teaching and learning about faith should stimulate excitement and enthusiasm for adults. We usually assume that education at the earliest ages and grade levels should be exciting and interesting, but we often lose sight of that goal for ourselves. We may hesitate to disrupt the so-called serious nature of learning.[6] Similarly, we may be somewhat apprehensive about the generation of too much excitement in our church classrooms, hallways, and chapels because the presence of such energy signals a transgression of boundaries. Learning about our faith and relationship with God, we think, is supposed to be a serious matter.

Faithfully approaching and transgressing boundaries opens and expands our relationship with God; it is not intended to be an excuse for violence or disregard of one another or God's creation. Transgressing boundaries can be frightening for some people, though, so enthusiasm and excitement must be balanced with appropriate public decorum and professional ethics. Pastoral leaders can facilitate opportunities for people to develop insights and awareness, or what Carl Jung calls "ah-hah" moments, that don't require revelation of intimate details. Exercises in which people reflect on, or write about, their responses without expressing them verbally fosters these moments while maintaining a calmer level of excitement. Such practices illustrate a means to support faithful transgression. When we transgress faithfully we

Holy irreverance

allow for the healthy presence of emotions and feelings within contexts that have established ethical and principled guidelines.

With appropriate boundary safeguards in place, faith communities grow in *agape* and *eros* through play practices. *Agape* is unconditional love, the love of God that we seek in faith to respond to and enact in relationship with others. *Eros* causes more trouble, being the love that Rita Nakashima Brock calls "the power of our primal interrelatedness." Erotic power heals and mends human relationships as it "creates and connects hearts, involves the whole person in relationships of self-awareness, vulnerability, openness, and caring."[7] *Eros* beckons us into intimate relationship with one another; it is love that sparks laughter and pleasure; love that dances until dawn. *Eros* delights in the body. We have too frequently, though, limited the definition of *eros* to the physical, sexual intimacy between married partners. *Eros* in play allows growth in healthy, life-giving, and life-affirming ways. An engaged, and therefore radical, leadership and educational practice takes seriously the role of *eros,* and incorporates passion in learning that subverts the mind/body split and allows people to be whole as well as wholehearted.[8] *Eros* thus infuses faith with compassion.

Through the play of *eros* in community, we touch and connect with one another. Congregations engage positive and faithful *eros* in the ritual of footwashing, as we bathe the feet of our sisters and brothers in Christ after the servanthood example of Jesus. Youth group leaders support the expression of *eros* through group hugs and sharing around sensitive subjects during regular meetings. Caregivers reach out and touch the hands and rub the backs of those who in pain or anguish. *Eros* also delights as members shriek and cheer together at a joint gathering of congregational choirs. *Eros* plays in the intense wrestlings of a Bible study group that convenes weekly to engage passionate narratives from the Hebrew scriptures and their connection to current life stories.

Eros has a rightful place in faith communities. When we allow for the positive expression of *eros*, we in essence de-eroticize it and in so doing familiarize ourselves with its complete meaning. We claim its power for learning and growth in our faith, learning that engages the whole person, mind and body, left brain and right brain. In Christian communities, in our playing together, we ignite *eros,* and in so doing teach our children and youth to recognize and respect its power. Given appropriate contexts and care within our faith, *eros* can be shaped and integrated, rather than diminished. Society needs positive and healthy ways to integrate *eros* as well. Church communities can become teachers and role models for the wider community when we do not fear or rigidly restrict *eros,* but recognize the powerful and positive force its energy has in building vibrant relationships.

Eros requires sound ethical guidelines because of the devastating effects on the lives of people and communities when leaders violate— often through sexual misconduct—the relationship between pastor and parishioner.[9] *Eros* can be a means of faithful transgression, only in so far as ethical guidelines and boundaries are maintained.

Play Fosters Embodied Knowing

As an educational and leadership practice, play emphasizes a participatory and engaged form of knowing, an embodied knowing. In play, we form relationships with others, without necessarily having an *understanding* of them. Play is a more free form kind of learning; so instead of teaching from principle to experience, we start from experience. In colloquial language, play is a way to educate outside the theological box. Our rational mind leads us to neatly categorize things, including people, ideas, and concepts. We may leap to premature closure, and miss the experience of that which does not fit our categories.

The Enneagram diagnostic tool, like other personality assessment tools, can be a valuable aid in helping understand human motivation.[10] It is important to remember, though, that this is personality tool. In this conceptual system, every person "fits" one of nine different dispositions. A colleague, trying desperately to use this tool to assess her colleagues in ministry, sighed in exasperation, "I have to figure out what number people are so I can understand them." Many of us try to understand others by using preexisting categories. Once we have fit a person into one of the nine boxes we assume that we have the basic outline of who that person is. Such tools can be useful for broadly illumining general patterns of human behavior, but can be problematic when we assume that a broad, arbitrary category of personality can help us understand the unique human being we encounter in the present moment.

Moving from understanding to encounter is a conceptual and experiential shift. We focus on being present with a person rather than trying to understand them. We pay attention to thoughts and feelings we are having, and use them to expand ways of staying in relationship with one another. Moving from understanding to encounter means we engage our intellects and our passions as we serve each other and God's world.

Playing in Sand

Playing in sand is good therapy and good education. A few simple guidelines can enhance the use of sandplay as a beneficial education practice with children, youth, and adults.[11] Sandplay therapy — or sandplay religious experience as I refer to it — offers a tactile, right-brain experience that can open some people to new awareness of their lives, including struggles, difficulties, and impasses. It is a particularly helpful exercise to access the deeper layers of experience and can be useful to reach people who are not comfortable in the verbal realm those who learn through touch and making associations. This play practice is well suited for people with disabilities since physical movement is not required.

There is a difference between sandplay therapy as practiced by licensed professionals and sandplay pastoral care education. While a pastoral psychotherapist might use this method to help a person to gain clarity about emotional conflicts, pastoral ministers have a slightly different goal in mind. Pastors committed to play methods in ministry want to expand beyond the use of words in order to include actual playing with concrete symbols and images. The method developed here is an educational tool that can help individuals and groups to access, and then to express, aspects of the nonrational mind.

For a session of sandplay, one will gather three hundred to five hundred miniature figures that can be placed in trays of sand. Some practitioners caution that more figures than this can be overwhelming for people. The sand trays themselves may have painted blue bottoms and sides to symbolize water or sky, and can be filled with different colors of sand to highlight the visual contrast with the objects. Note that red sand can provoke a rather intense emotional response in some people. The collection of figures, used to enact scenes, actual or psychic, may include representations of human beings or animals as well as a collection of houses, churches, trees, and so on.

In this practice, the educator does not occupy the role of the interpreter but rather that of observer/commentator. Learning is not imposed on participants, but they experience the freedom to learn what is important to them. Playful pastoral educators help facilitate the context in which this learning can occur. When we interpret another's inner experience, we take responsibility for naming and framing the experiences of the other person, and the language we use may or may not fit them. The interpreter makes connections between seemingly disparate aspects of another's experience, helping the person to see in a new way. By contrast the commentator acknowledges, describes, and reflects what is seen, taking care not to overstate meanings or make unhelpful references to the other person's life experience. We tread lightly with this work; we note associations and connections as we see them. Ultimately, the significance and meaning-making occurs between God and the person playing in the sand. The presence of an observer is important to the process by helping the person fully appreciate and "take in" the experience of playing in the sand. The observer may help make connective associations that we might not be able to make by ourselves. And they do so through a practice of observant noninterference (my phrase). Observers can note such aspects as:

- the placement of the figures in the sand in relation to other figures and objects;

- any feelings that the person expresses before, during, or after constructing the scene; and
- the player's own interpretation of the scene.

Participants are free to discover insights and lessons for themselves that will influence their faith and relationships with God.

We tread lightly with sandplay; we note associations and connections as we see them. Ultimately, the significance and meaning-making occurs between God and the person playing in the sand.

Play as Haggling in the Marketplace

Haggling in the marketplace is a form of play within intercultural immersion. International travel immersions and work trips can also be an invaluable means to develop relationships with God's people across the globe. Meaningful learning occurs in contexts in which people labor, study, and work together. Significant learning about another culture can also emerge from rather surprising and unexpected places. Haggling is an engaged form of faithful learning because the practice brings strangers into close and interactive relationship. Haggling is about creative give-and-take, a form of play in which respect of the other person is as important as attainment of a goal. Haggling as a faithful play practice teaches Christians to meet the face of God in the marketplace.

Bargaining can be a rather unsettling experience for westerners who are unfamiliar with the practice. But one of my own experiences in a Chinese marketplace turned out to be playful, even as it seemed to be very serious at times. I was elated to find a hanging scroll imprinted with evocative language of an ancient poem I remembered from my years studying Chinese, so I inquired about the price. Thinking the request was too high given my knowledge of what other vendors were asking, I politely made a counteroffer. The saleswoman offered me what she called a "friendship price." Still thinking the price to be too high, I gave my final offer and then walked away. Eventually, this price was accepted but the vendor made a number of gestures indicating that she had sold the piece significantly below its value. A companion told me that I had driven a hard bargain! I felt somewhat guilty until I realized the rule of the marketplace: vendors would not sell an item for less than it originally cost.

Bargaining and haggling stretch the experience of many U.S. Christians. We sometimes unhelpfully restrict the places where God can be found, and meaningful connections made. As a practice of faithful play, haggling brings us into close relationship with the basic needs of life and could be beneficially fostered in our culture. Pastoral leaders can encourage this practice as a means to develop interpersonal relationships. This give and take, what philosopher Hans Gadamer calls the to-and-fro movement, takes place between at least two people or groups. Bargaining, in an intercultural immersion context, is a form of play when the to-and-fro movement is recognized as a significant part of the interchange. The actual purchase is only one aspect of the encounter.

A colleague lends further cultural and theological interpretation to the experience of bargaining and haggling.

> *While on a trip to India, my colleague bargained on the price of an item; following the exchange and purchase, the merchant returned the equivalent of $5. Assuming the lens of a cultural anthropologist, my colleague interpreted this gesture to reveal several meanings. First, returning the token amount of money communicated that the merchant enjoyed the process of the interaction. Second, the gesture signaled that the bargaining over the item was not completely about the purchase of an item, but also about the fostering of a relationship. The merchant was indicating that he valued the relationship itself. Haggling and bargaining, as theological play in the marketplace, does exactly this: it values people and processes as much as the ends.*

Pastoral leaders can help people navigate through the intercultural experience of travel immersions by interpreting these dynamics of play. What on the surface seems to be of most value — the purchase of an item — is actually only a part of the experience. Learning to play in these environments is to see for ourselves and to help others see that more happens than we initially perceive. As we make this shift in understanding, we come to value a playful theology, one in which we intellectually know as well as experientially embrace the importance of fostering kindred relationships in all that we do, both within the church walls and far outside of them.

Intercultural Work/Play Projects

Intercultural mission and work projects represent one "outside the walls of the church" way of building meaningful relationships and fostering growth in faith. Young adults as well as others are often eager to put their faith into action. The young as well as the older adults want to make a difference in the world through community acts of justice and mercy. Working with others becomes play; it's more fun than working alone, and we learn about God, ourselves, and others in the process. Congregational programs organized for hands-on mission projects as well as service in the community embody playful theology.

A playful perspective can help when things go awry. A group of college students on a work project during spring break had hearts larger than their skill base. One day, they worked diligently on several minor projects around a home including the fixing of a fence, repairing window frames and painting. The family had experienced job loss and illness, leaving them with virtually no resources to maintain their modest home. By day's end, the students left almost as much damage as they helped repair. A cracked window pane and an awkward-leaning fence post were among the most visible signs of the students' work. Still, the family expressed appreciation for the labor of love. All throughout the day, members of the family and the students had shared personal stories. The elderly grandfather made quite an impression on the young adults as he freely expressed his own life philosophy, saying that even though he had been monetarily poor throughout his life he still had a "satisfied mind and heart." These words came as a meaningful gift, making a lasting impression on the students. The words came as a living reminder of what a playful theology offers: the engagement in mutually beneficial relationships, grounded in the awareness of God's love. We will be constantly surprised by what we receive when our intention is to give.

Play, as an experience of faith, can take many forms in congregational education. The many possibilities are limited only by our imaginations. Pastoral leaders can make these experiences possible and provide theological interpretation and reflection. Play is one way to make faith meaningful within a wide variety of contexts to people in the pews who navigate intellectual and emotional challenges at work, in the family, and in society. Pastoral leaders need to respect the hesitation and reluctance that people may have about the educational experiences described in this chapter. Playful communities make for playful people; if the church is to benefit from creative and playful endeavors, then leaders need to create environments and support initiatives that welcome and celebrate creative play.

Questions for Personal and Group Reflection

1. What does the concept of "voice" mean to you? Was there ever a time when you did not have a voice? How did you discover or develop it? What kind of learning environment is most conducive for you to develop voice?

2. Recall an instance in your personal or professional life when a meaningful dialogue with other people changed your perspective. What was that experience like? Were you initially afraid? Apprehensive? Enthusiastic? What did you learn through the encounter that influences your current practice?

3. Who has served as an educational role model or mentor for you in your development as a leader? What qualities do you most value in this person?

4. Describe experiences in your current setting in which children have the opportunity to learn through play. How can similar educational practices be developed for adult learners and leaders?

5. How risk-willing or risk-averse are you? How about your community? Reflect on ways in which comfort with regard to risks influences the ability to learn and teach others about play.

6. Consider your own life history and educational experience in relation to making mistakes. What messages did you receive in your family, church, and schools about mistakes? How have mistakes shaped your growth as a person and as a leader?

7. Implement a play day with your organization. Reflect on the value of taking Sabbath time together as a community. What elements can be put into place so that people could have a play day, an opportunity for team and community building, on a regular basis?

8. What rules or boundaries do you claim for yourself or others than can limit leadership learning opportunities? What would it take for you to "faithfully transgress" these boundaries in order to explore new possibilities for ministry?

9. Plan an opportunity for a group in the congregation — including staff and lay people — to use an assessment tool such as the Enneagram or the Myers-Briggs Personality Inventory. Discuss the insights gleaned from the exercise.

10. Go to a playground and play. (It's like entering one big sand-tray!) Pay attention to the apparatuses you like most. What are the thoughts and feelings you have in this place? Ask others to reflect what they see in the patterns of your play. What do you learn about leadership in this setting?

5 Leadership as Playful Creative Adventure

It is the thing that does not "fit" which lures and leads us on.

— Maria Harris
Teaching and Religious Imagination

I learned a lesson about leadership early in my childhood from the game "follow the leader." Selected as leader, I lined up my friends behind me for a trek through the neighborhood. I stepped forward and turned my head to make sure others were following. Immediately, I walked directly into a huge wooden plank used by a neighbor to support his boat and earned a gash in my forehead that required several stitches. Several insights about leadership are revealed in this incident: leaders and communities pay a price for not paying attention to where we are going. Others will not always point out obstacles. And the practice of leadership itself, while weighted with responsibility for organizations and other people, can also be conceived of as a form of skillful play.

Creative leadership, like "follow the leader," is an adventure. Unlike the childhood game, though, the playful nature of adult leadership is not nearly as simple as following the person in front. The kind of religious leadership I refer to draws on intellectual mastery as well as a honed capacity for creative and emotional intelligence. Development of true and authentic selfhood—for ourselves and for members of congregations we lead—may place us in tension with predominant cultural norms and expectations. We risk embarking on this creative adventure in response to the God who calls communities to vibrant life.

Playfully creative pastoral leaders foster the valuable qualities of imagination, intuition, speculation, and intellectual daring.[1] Such leadership synthesizes adult and child-like qualities in an effort to open minds and hearts to the wonder and challenge of God: adult in that we recognize and honor ambiguity, and child-like in that we never lose sight of amazing things. Creative religious leaders embody the union of complexity and simplicity of which Oliver Wendell Holmes reflects: "For the simplicity on this side of complexity, I would not give you a fig. But for the simplicity on the other side of complexity, for that I would give you anything I have."[2]

A Theology for Leadership[3]

While playful leaders are neither revolutionists nor evolutionists, playful leadership builds on theory that recasts the previously understood distinctions between revolution and evolution.[4] Evolutionary theory is viewed as a single line of an organic process through history, with the past linked in a coherent manner to the future. Revolutionary theory marks an abrupt disconnection with or upheaval from history in order to chart a new course in a social-cultural process. Contemporary pastoral leaders must be equipped with a theological leadership perspective that builds on an understanding of how change process actually occurs in the world as we know it (evolution), in order to be radical stewards of faith in God's world (revolution). Playful leadership theory and practices explored in this chapter aim to do just this.

The Stature of Religious Leadership

Effective pastoral leadership, which is primarily about developing relationships with people, requires the building up of what Bernard Loomer calls persons of "S-I-Z-E," or stature of soul.[5] Consider Loomer's words:

> By size, I mean the stature of a person's soul, the range and depth of his love, his capacity for relationships. I mean the volume of life you can take into your being and still maintain your integrity and individuality, the intensity and variety of outlook you can entertain in

the unity of your being without feeling defensive or insecure. I mean the strength of your spirit to encourage others to become freer in the development of their diversity and uniqueness. I mean the power to sustain more complex and enriching tensions. I mean the magnanimity of concern to provide conditions that enable others to increase in stature.[6]

Stature has love and regard for self and continually seeks what I call the "enlargement of the other" (see chapter 7). Playful leadership as creative adventure, therefore, is stature-growing work and celebrates numbers of people as well as increased relationship depth in the community.

In play we can move from the realm of possibilities into actuality.[7] While God's future holds boundless possibilities, it is through creative action that these possibilities can become actualized in ministry. Play frees us to step outside of comfort zones and habitual patterns for new action. God's possibilities are made known through a variety of means — thoughts, beliefs, values, attitudes, and dreams — to beckon us toward the new heaven and new earth. It is important to pay playful attention to them!

Soul Leadership in the Midst of Institutional Change

As the heart of religious leadership, stature is needed to withstand changes and challenges facing the institutional church. One imaginative way to foster soulful leadership is to pay attention to dreams, as significant biblical characters of old did. Remembering, reflecting, and acting on dreams is a powerful means to access God's wisdom and guidance. Revealed in imagery that may at first seem cryptic, we begin to unravel a mysterious puzzle as we listen carefully to the messages in dreams. Working with dreams serves a personal and congregational benefit: it directs our focus to metaphors, senses, intuitions, and feelings that might otherwise go unheeded by rational thought alone.[8] This soulful practice lures us into the reflective posture of stopping from ordinary busyness, looking for unusual or new signs and clues, and listening to submerged or dismissed voices. Such a soul practice reclaims a part of our religious heritage, by following in the footsteps of characters in the Bible, leaders who responded to God's prompting.

One minister reports a dream of walking through a church sanctuary, a grand and beautiful cathedral with stone walls, intricate stained glass windows, and fine wood pews. Suddenly the walls collapse inward. Under the dust and rubble, only the foundation remains.

Given this dream image we can ask:

- What is crumbling?
- Where do we stand in the midst of this change?
- What within our soul, personally as well as collectively, remains in spite of the crumbling structure?

The beauty of God's church, conveyed in the paradoxical image of the dream, is captivating. We are committed to the vision of the communion of the church and the reign of God's realm, the sure foundation, in spite of crumbling structures. This dream will resonate with pastoral leaders, who remain faithful to their churches and denominations, even through the pain of disillusionment and change. Leadership in unsettled times of decay or decline, represented in a dream of collapsing walls raises questions: How does personal or congregational energy get consumed in ways that lead to further decline? In what ways can our focus and attention be shifted to enlarge the soul of the community?

Play and Stature

Play develops transformative leaders of stature and moral clarity who engage communities with issues of deep significance.[9] Through play we need not do things the way they've always been done.[10]

Play contributes to an increase in stature in several ways:

- Play is fully immersed in the immediacy of the present. Leaders cannot help usher in God's new future for the community if they are unwilling to be *here* now.

- Play orients us differently to reality by bringing us to experience the event before we intellectually categorize the event.
- Play cultivates our innate capacity for intelligence.[11] Pastoral leaders increase their effectiveness in relating with people as they develop skill in strengthening their primary forms of intelligence as well as developing other intelligences.
- Play awakens, or reawakens, the passion for God's call in our lives. As acclaimed theological author Frederick Buechner writes, "The place God calls you to is the place where your deep gladness and the world's deep hunger meet."[12]
- Through play, we practice trusting God, ourselves, and others. Soulful character is developed because we face the possibility of failure, but it is here that we discover the Divine arms ready to catch us.

The Play of Power in Leadership

The use of power in pastoral leadership is confusing for ministers. Effective and playful religious leaders use power to contribute to building up of the entire community. Shared power in community, or what Bernard Loomer calls *relational power,* is "the capacity to influence others and to be influenced by others,"[13] as opposed to *unilateral power,* or "the capacity to influence, guide, adjust, manipulate, shape, control, or transform the human or natural environment in order to advance one's own purposes."[14] Unilateral power is identified as hierarchical or patriarchal power, and referenced in the New Testament as *katakuriero,* the power to become master over another. This form of power constricts the freedom of the other.

> **Relational power** *is "the capacity to influence others and to be influenced by others."* **Unilateral power** *is "the capacity to influence, guide, adjust, manipulate, shape, control, or transform the human or natural environment in order to advance one's own purposes."*

Relational power entails the ability to give and to receive, to affect others and to be affected by them; this power emerges within relational ministry and supports it. The sharing of power in relationship with others requires pastoral leaders to have a greater sense of self-confidence and trust. Viewed as "weak" from the position of dominant culture, relational power reflects the heart of servant leadership echoed in the gospels.[15] The ability to influence and be influenced by others in thought and feeling reflects a strength of capacity in pastoral leadership.

Leadership always involves the use of power; so the question is not whether to use it, but how to engage power faithfully and effectively. Unilateral power places others in a dependent position and often derives psychologically from a place of fear and insecurity. In contrast, relational power inherently draws others into conversation through the interdependence and mutuality of shared power. The result is participants benefit: vital and adaptive ministries thrive. Play used to tease, belittle, denigrate, or diminish people is destructive and should not be tolerated; it indicates an immature playground mentality, not mature leadership.

Leadership always involves the use of power; so the question is not whether to use it, but how to engage power faithfully and effectively.

Religious leaders are entrusted with the responsible use of power, the dynamic that the New Testament refers to as *eksousia*, the power that enhances the freedom of choice and capability. It serves to bring about *dunamis*, making space for the power of God to emerge.

A Playful Image of God: Serendipitous Creativity

How would our leadership practices and ministries look if we imagined God as the Being of Creative Play or Serendipitous Creativity?[16] As we image God differently, so may we come to new understanding of the possibilities for our roles as pastoral leaders. This vision of God as Serendipitous Creativity supports a pastoral theology of playful leadership.

God as "Serendipitous Creativity" differs markedly from God as a parent to humanity as children. Such a shift in our view of God can influence our thinking about leadership. If God by God's very nature shares creatively and lovingly in the constructive power of creation, then we might free ourselves to participate in this endeavor through our ministerial practices. Serendipitous Creativity invites us into responsive and responsible relationship to the Divine, with one another, and with the whole of the "magnificent intricate web of life on earth."[17] While the creativity of God yearns for the greatest possible good for all, we also recognize that creative human efforts have destructive as well as constructive purposes and results. God as Serendipitous Creativity hopefully expands our theological view of pastoral leadership and draws us to playful, creative efforts on behalf of all.

To name God as Serendipitous Creativity, as Kaufman does, is not meant to imply that all creativity is of the same order or magnitude. While human creativity and leadership is connected to God as Creativity, God alone is the primary source of creativity. We create because God is creative. So, in Christian community, we worship God as Source of creation, and as Source of our creative selfhood and creative endeavors. Why does this matter? In this vision of ministry as play, we begin to see ourselves as significant agents in the process of creating in relation with the Creative One. Pastoral leaders who value Serendipitous Creativity will more likely embody and lead others toward appreciation, delight, and surprise in God.

Leadership as Creative Adaptability

Creative and playful leadership intentionally harnesses and builds on the energy of that which does not necessarily "fit," recognizing that "misfittings" may be signs of God's active presence in calling a community to its authentic livelihood. Playful leadership does, however, take initiative and respond creatively to challenges by helping communities to embody their deepest values and develop new practices for enabling creative life. This process of "adaptive work" stimulates vitality in congregations.[18]

Other aspects of adaptability are highlighted when viewed through the lens of play. Brian Sutton-Smith develops a perspective on play that he names "adaptive variability,"[19] which has the inherent characteristics of quirkiness, redundancy, and flexibility.[20] Religious leaders must help communities through change, and the manner they go about this is important. Quirkiness implies that not everything fits a set pattern, and anomaly or difference should receive attention. Redundancy produces an "extra capacity" for whatever is necessary. In ministry, the same message appears in multiple places such as the newsletter, website, Sunday bulletin. Redundant communication frees leaders to focus more energy on developing new initiatives within the congregation or community instead of monitoring the conflict that emerges when people are left "out of the loop." Flexible pastoral leaders stay open to change, responsive to learning new skills, and aware that a variety of practices builds strong ministries.

Effective Practice Techniques

Effective pastoral leaders learn to minister in both technical and adaptive situations. A technical situation usually has a predetermined response. An adaptive situation requires multiple and complex responses. These situations usually pose the greatest challenge and stimulate a higher degree of satisfaction for ministers and congregations.

Leaders are most effective in adaptive situations as they engage the following strategies:

- Identify the adaptive challenge; focus on a proper diagnosis of the situation and the nexus of connected issues.
- Keep the level of distress within a tolerable range for doing adaptive work. Some level of tension is healthful for persons and systems to engage in useful work.
- Focus attention on ripening issues and not on stress-reducing distractions. Identify the issues that deserve attention.

- Give the work back to the people, but at a rate they can manage; this requires that persons in leadership know when and how frequently work should be delegated.

- Protect voices of leadership with no authority. Those who ask "hard questions" and give expression to contradictions have an important contribution to make.[21]

Adaptive leaders balance between two possible extremes: Challenge people too quickly or press them too hard and they are likely to accuse the leader of failing to meet their needs for stability and constancy. Challenge people too slowly and they might blame the person in authority for making no progress. Leaders walk this tightrope, or in the words of Heifetz, stand on the "razor's edge."[22] As the phrase suggests, those who exercise authority will eventually experience the pain of getting cut. In the same way, those who exercise playful and creative leadership may be just as likely as other ministers to experience difficult challenges in ministry. Leadership conceived this way helps pastors frame ministry and leadership in terms of being flexible in meeting the next challenge instead of guarding the status quo. Playful leadership, like adaptive work, places emphasis on developing capacity and means to respond to and initiate change on behalf of enriching the congregation's morale and mission.

Cultivating Facilitating Environments

Playful pastoral leaders are primarily responsible for exercising appropriate power and authority through principled and creative practices that change and adapt to the circumstances. Ministers, as caretakers of God's beloved community, contribute substantially to what Winnicott calls the "facilitating environment" for growth and change.[23] In the earliest stages of human development, the facilitating environment involves the way an infant is touched and in every way cared for so that trust and confidence in life develops. Pastoral leaders are likewise responsible for creating conditions and contexts in which people may grow in trust and respond to God's call in their lives. A reliable environment allows children the space to grow and develop without threat and harm. By extension, such an environment allows adults the space to express themselves free from undue criticism or rebuke. Ministers create optimal facilitating environments by establishing support structures as well as space for experimentation—for journeying, falling, testing, and standing up again to take the next steps—that grow healthy and vibrant faith communities. This balance and negotiation between exerting power and not taking too much power guides without manipulating and fosters vision without controlling it.

Ministers create optimal facilitating environments by establishing support structures as well as space for experimentation—for journeying, falling, testing, and standing up again to take the next steps—that grow healthy and vibrant faith communities.

Playful Leadership Practices

Playful leadership practices reflective of Serendipitous Creativity balance constancy and stability with new and innovative practices. Like the church's central ritual of worship, these practices focus on the "deepening of the faith life."[24] Creative church rituals build on, challenge, and expand the stories of faith in ways that enhance ministry.[25] As scripted yet open-ended play, rituals bridge the known and unknown and allow people to enter the sacred tension between "reality" as it is and God's imaginative "vision" for what it could be. The following playful leadership practices are forms of healthy ritual[26] that help to negotiate the transitional space between "what is" and "what could be," in efforts to live in God's community.[27]

Venturing Out and Returning Back

Transformative leaders travel beyond personal and cultural boundaries in order to understand other people and explore their stories. This form of venturing out and returning home is what several authors refer to as "a good pilgrimage."[28] Pilgrimages are akin to what Gadamer describes as the to-and-fro movement inherent in play.[29] Going out to and returning from home to tell the story about the experience is an aspect of play.

A personal story of pilgrimage, venturing out and returning home, illustrates the value of this practice for pastoral leadership.

I met Annie when I was a pastor of a parish in rural Upstate New York. As the manager of the Organic Foods market in Oneonta, she greeted everyone from behind the counter, at the back of the store. Annie assisted customers, stocked shelves, labeled packages, and tallied charges. Often, she made helpful suggestions on products to purchase, not based on making a big sale but to match a customer's needs. Annie herself walked with a limp, because one leg was shorter than the other. The success of this small business depended, in no small measure, on Annie's care-filled assistance in helping persons with the "incidentals" of their life.

An urgent matter in the parish brought me to the health food store in a moment of pastoral desperation. In anticipation of a Christmas Eve baptism, I was informed me that the previous minister anointed babies with frankincense and myrrh after celebrating the sacrament of baptism. The church leaders wanted the practice to continue. Unsure of where to purchase frankincense and myrrh, I ventured to the local Christian bookstore. The woman in the shop graciously, yet firmly, said that they did not carry that sort of thing and suggested I try the health food store down the block.

So, I ended up in front of Annie's counter. When she heard what I was looking for, she laughed through her words, "You mean you don't have a Presbyterian supply shop for that sort of thing?" The health food store did not stock these oils either, but Annie made a call and asked if I would be comfortable going to a New Age shop to get the oils. I purchased the oils and my source remained a secret between Annie and me. Our Christmas Eve baptism was a meaningful ritual, and the baby carried aroma of ancient biblical oils.

Creative play is implemented through searching outside the defined boundaries of the congregation and incorporating insights and nontraditional resources. Reflecting on the experience inspires future creativity.

This pilgrimage into the New Age store was needed in order to provide the ritual leadership that this community expected. Lessons from the story can be easily overlooked. So much goes on beyond the scenes of pastoral leadership. In this case, effective pastoral initiative made possible a meaningful celebration of the sacrament of baptism that connected to the Christmas story. The ritual of playful pilgrimage embodies flexibility: in creative preparation for ministries of the church and in care-filled integrity, we play with the rituals. Creative leaders look for ways to incorporate what initially may appear quirky into the practice of ministry.

Asking the Impertinent Question

Churches and people who are open to growth recognize the pertinent value of impertinent or seemingly misfit questions. Through asking them and listening for response we become God's distinctive people and communities.[30] Creative pastoral leaders help people and congregations to ask questions that they may be hesitant or unwilling to voice; response to such questions often leads to meaningful action. Impertinent questions should never be used to embarrass, harass another person, nor violate emotional or physical boundaries.

Creative pastoral leaders help individuals and congregations adapt to new situations by asking the impertinent question, a redundant practice that gives voice to thoughts that probably have already occurred to others. Leaders themselves can ask the question or make space for others to ask; in a family it might be the marginalized or scapegoated member, or in a committee it might be the person who asks the "difficult" questions. In a pastoral conversation, it might be the question that occurs over and over again in the mind of the minister but the other person is not asking. People may consider asking the impertinent question to be rude, displeasing, or intrusive, but it helps instigate change by opening avenues of inquiry or courses of action for individuals and congregations.

Pastoral leaders who carefully and sensitively ask impertinent questions help deepen relationships with God and one another. In a pastoral conversation,[31] the impertinent question allows pastors to get to the heart of a matter. Consider, for example, a family gathered at the bedside of a loved one who is dying, as they dance tentatively around the subject of death because of discomfort or fear. The dying loved one, unsure or unable to broach matters dear to the heart, may benefit from a gentle prod from the pastor. The pastor might ask any number of questions or simply ask those gathered what is on their minds or if there is anything they would like to share with one another. Impertinent questions could include: "Are there things left unsaid or unexpressed among you that you would like to say? Or at the right time in the conversation, asking questions such as, "Do you have any particular wishes for your memorial service that you would like us to remember?" "Is there anything you would particularly like to have us do at your memorial service?" Once when I asked this question, a congregant said she wanted a liturgical dance performed in her honor. Asking the impertinent question, whether in a pastoral moment such as this or in some other context of ministry, opens space for people to respond and for the appropriate ritual to emerge.

Creating Relational Time

The leadership practice of "creating time"[32] for developing and sustaining relationships in community is a valuable misfit practice, especially in western cultures where time is often viewed as a commodity to be purchased or traded rather than a sacred invitation for relational living. The practice has become something of a misfit because of its increasing marginalization. In the African-American church, creating time for nurturing relationships in community occurs when people come together at the welcome table of a church potluck. Those who have experienced the wounding effects of racism gather in sacred relational space to recognize and affirm one another and to love themselves and God.[33] People extend welcome and compassion to one another around the tables of abundant and sumptuous food, sharing experiences of difficulty and challenge as well as joy and celebration. At the welcome table, congregants create time to play together, nurturing soul and spirit.

Keeping Sabbath is one significant way to create time. We offer God the gift of our time as we focus on worship instead of work, and self-care instead of self-importance. In the sacrament of Sabbath keeping, we remember who and whose we are and dedicate our lives to God on an experiential level. In the free space of Sabbath we come to know more intimately that God tends our souls with gentle care that restores us to life. Keeping Sabbath in cultures driven by demands and expectations is difficult, but it is a spiritual practice that honors the rhythm of God's creation with a time and season for all things. Leaders who commit to regular Sabbath practice, and encourage others to do so as well, counter the grinding cultural expectation that we should work until we drop.

Improvisational Leadership

Leadership though improvisation is a playfully creative practice that can be more effective in ministry that we realize.

A church executive who administers a large residential community for retired religious leaders faces many challenges in his ministry of the ongoing management of a large staff and the recruitment of healthcare professionals to serve in this long-term care facility. This church administrator recalls how methods of study as a student informed his early practices as a ministerial leader. Studiously he would spend hours rewriting lecture notes in an effort to learn the material. With all this effort, he still was only earning Bs and Cs in his courses. He eventually discovered an effective way of learning. Instead of overly focusing on learning the material, he states, "I learned to be less driven and rigid about my study habits. As I relaxed, I started to get As in my courses."[34]

The new method of learning and leadership included the following steps:

- letting go of internal pressure;
- recalling essential information; distilling the main points; and
- making connections with already known information.

This church executive feels sheepish about his improvisational style of leadership, even as he intuitively knows its effectiveness for ministry. As the director of a large organization, sometimes he still has no idea what he will do or be required to do in any given situation. A decision or plan will, "just come to me" during a meeting or a conversation. Far from being capricious or arbitrary, this practice requires preparation and skill, or what Csikszentmihalyi calls the "creativity that comes to prepared minds."[35]

Leadership improvisation is an advanced and creative skill that benefits ministry. Sometimes we reflect negatively on improvisation as "making something up," "by the seat of the pants," or "off the cuff." Improvisation as a skillful leadership practice is a form of play that allows ministers to exercise what Dykstra calls pastoral imagination.[36] Rather than apologizing for this practice we would do well to recognize its significance for leadership. Improvisation as a leadership practice builds on our ability to engage actively in other practices that support professional response: continuing education seminars, advanced reading, consultation with colleagues. Creative and playful leadership is improvisational as it builds from an increasing base of known skills and knowledge, and continually stretches toward the unknown.

Pushing the Edges of Creative Leadership

Imagination is the only limit on the possibilities for creative ministerial leadership. Many practices build on the concept of adaptive play as a way of developing ministries within a congregation and for engaging with the wider community. Consider the following playful adaptive ventures as prompting for your own ministry.

- Websites for ministerial leadership ideas: Scott Cormode, a scholar in the field of religious leadership education, has developed a Web site conceived of as "a learning playground for growing leaders"[37] that sparks innovative ideas for ministry. Web site information, including pastoral vignettes, relevant literature, reflective questions, and case studies, helps pastoral leaders fuel their own ministries based on online interaction with others. *more present in the moment*
- Pastoral weblogs for congregational communication: Pastoral leaders are using the internet as a way to reinvent the concept of the church newsletter. Instead of a document that arrives in mailboxes, a pastoral weblog allows pastors to communicate with congregants and others through regular commentary, including responses to theological questions in relation to events current in peoples' lives.

- Technology that brings the Seminary to the Church: the Wesley Ministry Network[38] offers prepared courses for congregants with video instruction, workbooks, regular email updates, and leaders' guides. Congregations benefit from current scholarship and recognized leaders addressing topics that matter to their lives of faith. Use of such resources supplements the local education offerings, especially of small congregations located in remote areas.

- Newspapers and Radio Programs: Print media and radio programs provide a venue to address what John Wesley called the world as congregation. When I served as a campus minister, the college newspaper ran a column authored by campus pastors, in rotation with the other members of the campus interfaith community, in which ministers addressed questions and issues of faith relevant to college students. Opinion articles by pastoral leaders appear regularly in newspapers, and religious radio programs reach audiences beyond the church walls.

Creatively playful pastoral leaders imagine the dream of a covenant community, living richly and deeply into God's realm, until we some day find ourselves at home in the arms of God, each and every one surrounded and known as the beloved. May pastoral leaders of stature help move God's people step-by-step in faith to embody the vision of prayerful and playful discipleship.

Questions for Personal and Group Discussion

1. Name a religious ritual that you have engaged in that has been beneficial, which you don't include in your current context. Consider the reasons for this.

2. What attempts at creative improvisation have you employed in your ministry context within the last year? What has been effective? What has not been so effective?

3. Consider the components — resources, people, programs — that need to be put into place to make the holding environment of your congregation nurturing of current members and inviting to newcomers. Where might you encounter resistance? What pastoral plans need to be put into place to honor the resistance and still move forward?

4. Reflect on the dimensions of how power is exercised in your leadership context. What policies, procedures, or practices can be changed or enhanced in order to influence relational power?

5. Sit quietly. What images surface when you reflect on God as Creative Serendipity? How does this theological image shape your understanding of leadership practices?

6. Evaluate your current community or context in relation to its ability to change and adapt. Name concrete possibilities, however significant or insignificant, that might help to enhance adaptability.

7. Reflect on a leadership practice that has engaged, or might engage, your congregation in the larger life of the community. How does reflection on play in the community shape or inform your understanding of what it means to engage in mission?

8. When was the last time you ventured outside the bounds of your regular commuting routine? Or outside the country, if you have the

available resources? What did you learn about leadership from the adventure?

9. Observe the language you and others use to describe "time." What kind of actions follow from this view? How can leadership practices help create time for community well-being?

10. Ask yourself an impertinent question about playful misfit leadership: What would your ministry look like if you were truly to become the leader God is calling you to become?

6 The Play of Pastoral Care

*God has identified with the misfits of the world and encourages us
to become marginal to structures that operate by standards of domi-
nation, injustice, and competition.*

— Letty M. Russell
Growth in Partnership

We might not ordinarily relate play with care, but such a connection
can be immensely valuable. Two different artistic expressions,
one drawn from music and the other from sculpture, help us make an
intuitive linkage between play and care. Such renderings give a sense
of how play infuses and informs practices of pastoral care.

As a child, I remember watching in wonder and amazement as my
great-grandmother played the piano without any music in front of her.
While able to read music, she preferred instead to play from memory.
Grandma Celia's talent with music developed early and she brought joy
to many people in the community as she played for dances throughout Amador County, California. Even well into her 90s with hearing
and eyesight diminishing, Celia would sit at the piano as her fingers
would dance across the keys. Her soul was full of music that she had
learned to play by ear. When I got older and took piano lessons myself,
I learned firsthand the difficulty of improvisational music playing. This
early experience left a lasting impression and stimulated my interest
in finding a creative expression for this important capacity.

A community foundation was formed in Claremont, California in response to a tragic event. A young African-American male was killed by a Caucasian police officer in the course of a routine traffic stop. The foundation wisely adopted a mission to foster projects that develop community dialogue and unity. John Fisher, a 1969 graduate of the city's only high school and a master craftsman in marble carving, was chosen for a project that would involve the whole community.[1] Unlike many artists who carve based on a model or blue-print of the image they intend to re-present, John begins by chipping away at the stone in order to "discover" the form that lies within. The completed art piece also contains areas of the original rock's rough surface as a visual re-minder whence the images inside have emerged. The form discovered in this particular slab of marble depicted a *bearded* elderly Caucasian *man* playing a musical instrument with a young woman of African-Asian features looking over his shoulder. Within several months of completion, vandals chipped away pieces of the image, and left cigarette-burn marks on the surface of the marble. Many people in the community felt hurt and angered by this violation of common property. In response, the foundation invited John Fisher, who graciously agreed, to restore the image, and it now depicts an elderly *woman* playing a musical instrument with the younger woman over-looking her shoulder.

These artistic expressions help capture sensitivities and sensibilities beneficial for care of people and communities. Each leaves us with an impression of a process that can be richly engaging while soulful and healing. Such a method of care shares characteristics with improvisational music and sculpting as it assumes a habit of mind that says, "Let's see what will emerge," without needing an entire blueprint. Rather than isolated and individualistic, these artistic images portray care that is internally connected and outwardly directed.

A pastoral theology of play helps pastoral leaders to "play by ear," to trust the music of the soul, and to sculpt in order to discover the image within the stone. Expression of creative play and its possibilities in ministry emerges from the theological vision of the creativity of

God that we briefly explored in the previous chapter. In this chapter, we explore how play cultivates misfit wisdom for ministry that enables practicing creative presence in the pastoral care ministries of the church.

Cultivating Misfit Pastoral Theological Wisdom

Pastoral leaders learn to care for a wide diversity of people in communities with many different needs and expectations. They rely on gathered theoretical and experiential wisdom in order to express a healing word or embody a care-filled presence. Theological reflection in actual communities can be anything but orderly and neat. The interplay of critical thought and open hearts provides local pastors as pastoral theologians with valuable tools for care ministries: pastors bring precise and reasoned thought to the task of helping people through challenges of faith in the shifting terrain of daily life.

I share with Alastair Campbell, a Scottish pastoral theologian, the vision of evoking images from the biblical texts to name the acts and qualities of care ministries.[2] One such image is that of the holy fool. We may prefer not to claim this gauche, disheveled, tragicomic figure as the image of our ministry. As a metaphor for the soul's interior life, though, the fool is a representative of valuable qualities: simplicity, loyalty, and prophecy.[3]

The folly of play opens people to simplicity of presence. Folly as simplicity helps people to rediscover the spontaneous aspects of personality that can be so easily lost or neglected in pursuit of adult wisdom.[4] The folly of play opens the personality to a new sense of loyalty that includes an adaptive and creative response to God and neighbor. Loyalty commits us to the ministry of the church and the vision of God or the beliefs of faith in spite of what others might say.[5] Holy fools are loyal to God with no assurance that they will get exactly what they want, but with full assurance that God brings abundant life in strangely surprising ways.

The folly of play also has a prophetic dimension. When they become oppressive or stifling to God's people, a prophet challenges social and church norms, conventions, and authorities. Pastoral leaders as wise and holy fools encourage people to question assumptions and revise personal and institutional practices that do harm to self and others. The prophetic movement of play interacts constructively with "what already is" in order to bring about what "could be." Pastoral leaders foster the fool's healthy wisdom in order to enlarge the soul and stimulate what Jim Dittes calls the "re-calling, reforming, revisioning" process of ministry. Such creative effort makes space for the Holy Spirit's "boiling vitality."[6]

Caring for the Misfits: Communities and Transitions

As part of soul care, pastoral ministers lead communities through periods of transition as a way to provide care that is playfully adaptive to people and circumstances. Ministers as soul caregivers also tend the spirit of misfit congregations and the creative misfits within communities.

Misfit Practices and Events in the Congregation

Congregations are home to a variety of practices that differ by community and context. As a young pastor, I came to appreciate the significance that parishioners placed on activities such as church dinners, bazaars, auctions, ice cream socials, and strawberry festivals. I previously had assumed that these activities largely served the purpose of raising money and that my presence at such events was optional. But I made a habit of attending, and came to realize that as the minister I served as a diplomatic link between community and congregation, and that the events carried meaning beyond any fund-raising function they might have.

On most of these occasions I mingled with members of the congregation as well as people from the neighborhood or extended family of congregants. Seminary education did not prepare me for the role of pastoral diplomat, yet I discovered a theological framework to help give shape to these "other" church events.

Viewed through the lens of play, pastoral leaders may come to see and experience such church practices in a new light. Through periods of change, these activities allow the church to "play" in the community by providing space for people to interact with one another with relative freedom. While not diminishing the level of work that these events entail, I think the spirit of community involvement and connection is satisfying for everyone. These events promote spiritual growth as people experience the healing power of the "purpose-free fellowship" of the church.[7]

These events are occasions when those from the community can meet and interact with members of the congregation in a nonthreatening and not-overtly religious environment. Yet the situations present many opportunities for communicating a message. As pastor, I talked with family, friends, and neighbors who otherwise might never enter the church building. Often I attended to matters of pastoral concern, such as listening to the story of a person's illness or a family tragedy or providing a blessing for a birth or marriage. Without a theological framework for such church-community practices, we might assume that the pastor's role is relatively insignificant. Sacred ministry emerges as people interact and communicate freely; within this creative potential space, the church as community offers meaningful pastoral care.[8]

Caring for Misfits in Congregations

Play gives pastors a theological framework for interpreting the experience of misfit people within congregations. Often standing at the community's margins, these members are able to stay within organized Christian religious communities when pastors support their spiritual yearning to explore other traditions and practices and then return to the community with newfound insights. At coffee hour one Sunday, I overheard a snippet from a nearby conversation. One person declared with exasperation, "You just have to practice the religion in order to be a Christian." The other person responded by simply saying, "Yes, I agree, but some people don't like to participate in organized religion."

Today, many cultural and generational influences are reshaping the dynamics within organized religion. With the shifts in religious communities, play helps caregivers frame how to care for people at the margins as well as the center of the community. We face two choices: first, whether or not we want to minister at the margins; and second, assuming we do, how do we work within changing contexts theologically and creatively for the benefit of all God's people.

We care for misfits in congregations by embracing inclusive religious practices that allow congregants to explore practices drawn from both East and West. Traditional faith practices, such as participation in worship, Bible studies, mission opportunities, and prayer groups nurture many people in the congregation. Other practices enhance and support the Christian faith of some who stand on the edge of our congregations. A member may take a temporary leave from community worship to join a retreat on yoga, which focuses on energy movement in the body. We might consider ways to incorporate yoga or other health healing practices within the congregational care program.

Traditional faith practices nurture many people in the congregation. Other practices enhance and support some who stand on the edges.

Play as Care for Ritual

Play as sacred ritual may serve to carry persons and communities through transitions of life. It helps us to bridge the gaps between where we are and where we want to be, between where we stand and where we are moving. Just as ritual provides a sense of stability and structure in the midst of a constantly evolving and complex world, play emerges into its fullness in structured, yet nonrigid contexts. Play, like ritual, has its own particular nuances and stylizations; play may be most satisfying to the human psyche and soul when it is infused with complexity, intricacy, and repetition. Play as a ritual form can provide a bounded and care-filled space for people to bring their longings and hopes as well as their sorrow, wounds, and grief. We bring these selves as an offering, as one creative contribution to the transformation of the world. Play can hold the tensions of our personal and community life, and may help us re-create our experience.

A campus minister's practice is a good case illustration.

> *Toward the end of an emotionally and spiritually difficult semester that included the suicide of a student, a campus pastor gathered with a group of students. They shared a meal and a Bible study of the baptism of Jesus. This passage was chosen to highlight the theme that we, like Jesus, are God's beloved. After study and discussion, the pastor realized that an enactment of this spiritual experience was missing. After bringing several bowls of water to the group, the pastor explained that they would engage in anointing one another in symbolic recognition of God's love for each one. Each of the students then dipped fingers into the water and touched the head of the person sitting next to them, saying, "You are God's beloved." Weeks later the students were still commenting on the power of this ritual, and how they experienced God's care for them.*

In this example of creative pastoral practice, the campus minister adapted a ritual to involve students in an actual experience. In responding to this serendipitous impulse, the pastor recognized God's spirit at creative work in the moment. In subsequent Bible study sessions, the pastor made sure to anticipate and prepare for creative ritual activity and to stay open to new possibilities that God might reveal, recognizing that ritual need not occur the same way each time.

Care in the Midst of Crisis and Major Life Transitions

Through play, ministers care for others and themselves in times of national crisis. A dream image invites reflection in light of the tragic events of September 11, 2001: I observe a plane crash into a city center, and I know that everyone on the plane, and many people on the ground, had died. I walk through the city up some very steep hills toward home. Through the emotional difficulty and challenge of crisis,

God continues to call us to well-being and wholeness. Many pastoral leaders wrestle with how to help people reach home, a safe and grounded place, during times of community or national tragedy.

The image of going home, juxtaposed against the cultural context of terrorist attacks in Washington, D.C., and New York City, conveys a message: going home to play embodies the hope of God in an uncertain and war-torn world. Through play we encourage our souls to respond to God's vision for shalom. The journey toward 'home' is not a literal matter of going to our houses of dwelling, and locking the doors in fear to the outside world. But the playful nature of the pilgrimage, of venturing out to engage in ministries of care, is a gift to the world. By this I mean deep-hearted play — the kind that springs from our beings as a resounding affirmation of life and all its possibilities for fullness while completely recognizing of the horrors and pains that accompany life.

In our playing and ritual practice we may experience healing. Play may contribute to what Letty Russell calls the mending of creation, and what Judaism refers to as *tikkun olam*, the "healing of the earth."[9] Ministers must assume responsibility for creating a context of safe and nonthreatening relationships in which the healing power of play might emerge. Play contributes to healing because the relationships developed embrace the power and presence of pain while making room for the expression of new life. The following brief vignette illustrates the direction of pastoral play in ministry.

> *During the sniper attacks in the Washington area that eventually left 10 people dead and millions of people feeling like hostages in their own city, the seminary organized a care event. The leaders created a ritual space in which two things happened: people shared their feelings of fear and anxiety and considered ways to move forward in community. People expressed gratitude for simply having the space to come together. This event did not have the tenor of a playful space since people were feeling too emotionally raw and vulnerable for this to occur. But the creation of the ritual itself was a form of spontaneous play: the organizers sensed a need*

*in the community and opened a space for people to share their cares
and concerns before God and one another. The leaders did not
know, and could not anticipate, what would actually transpire in
this space. They trusted that the Spirit of God would lead the way.*

A seminarian with an outstanding singing voice who often shared
his gift of music during chapel services raised a question during a
pastoral care course, inquiring if it would be appropriate to sing at a
parishioner's bedside. Sharing of musical arts in pastoral care can be
meaningful practice of play for caregivers and care-receivers going
through major life transitions. Pastoral caregivers need to stay mindful
not to disturb others or highlight musical gifts for self-promotion. It
is also important to ask people's permission to sing in their presence.

The following pastoral care case study illustrates the interplay of
pastoral care through transition as story listening, story sharing, and
song. As a hospice chaplain, I visited with Ardell many times over the
course of the two years before she died.

*Ardell was a wonderful storyteller, and had the ability to regale
her family and friends with details of stories across the span of
her life. One memorable story recalled a camping trip with her
parents. They arrived at the campground late one night and as she
helped her father set up the tent, they could hear what sounded
like rocks or pebbles descending from a cliff. They didn't think
much more of it, but in the daylight, they noticed how incredibly
close to a cliff they had pitched the tent. Ardell would tell the story
with such drama and suspense that the listener could imagine being on the brink of that cliff.*

*At her memorial service, Ardell's grandson retold a few of his
grandmother's hallmark stories. Many in the congregation were
in tears as everyone together remembered hearing these beloved
stories.*

*In preparation for the memorial homily, and after the bulletins
had already been printed, I realized that a fitting way to remember Ardell — in addition to recalling snippets of her stories — was
to honor her gift as a storyteller. Ardell loved music, from the organ*

concerts at the church to the birds chirping outside her bedroom window, but always said she couldn't sing if her life depended on it. So, at the end of my homily, I sang a couple of stanzas from "I Love to Tell the Story," and then invited the community to join. The sanctuary seemed filled with a wonderful sense of mystery during this interlude. People commented afterward on the significance of that particular point in the liturgy, a playfully creative moment during a solemn and sacred service.

My pastoral task was to frame Ardell's stories with theological significance, sharing with the community the value of telling stories and the connection between the stories we tell and God's storytelling in and through our lives. Weaving this together with creative integrity reflects the playfully artistic movement of pastoral care that can deeply touch the heart. Singing the story in community played a powerful role.

Soulful Play Nurtures Everyday Spirituality

Pastoral leaders care for God's beloved misfits by teaching playful spiritual practices. We'll explore several of them: caring for contemplative prayer, creating a memory of play, and sparking laughter and humor.

Caring for Contemplative Prayer

Jacqueline and Christopher, married for more than two decades, sat across from one another on the couch one autumn evening just after their only son had left for college. Reflecting on how different life seemed since Elliot's leaving, Jackie mused, "I am feeling homesick, but how can I be homesick when I am already home?"[10] Many people wonder about feeling homesick when they are already home. Pastoral leaders may feel this spiritual longing for home even as we care for those who feel this yearning to be fully embraced in God's tender loving arms.

Contemplative prayer puts us in touch with the source of this longing. Father Thomas Keating, a teacher of contemplative prayer, suggests that it is a form of "divine therapy" that opens the human person to

.arger, vaster dimensions of two questions: Who am I? Where am I in relation to God, to myself, and to others?[11] Cultivating the practice allows us to enter inner silence and play deeply and soulfully before God with these significant questions. Play, as with prayer, is a care-filled, open disposition toward the ultimate questions of human life. In the quiet space of prayer, the heart reflects.

This practice of prayer cultivates within us the ability to live more openly and freely, to play into the unknown. Prayer can be a means of play, and in turn, play can be a form of embodied prayer. We care for the spiritual practice of prayer in order to know God for ourselves and to teach others.[12] Practicing contemplative prayer increases our capacity to serve as "interpathic" listeners, skilled in bridging differences in worldviews and experience, in a world where people long to be heard amidst the cacophony of overwhelming words.[13] It also increases the ability hear through the mental "chatter" that interferes with hearing the still, small of voice of God and the voices of one another. Prayer helps us know the frequency of our personal "static," so that we are less likely to be held captive to its power. Our minds continuously produce thoughts in the form of judgments, opinions, analyses about ourselves and other people. In fact, we think so much that we often assume that our thoughts comprise who we are. Silent prayer does not eliminate our production of thoughts, but it opens an internal "potential space" so we can hear the internal conversation of endless commentary for what it is. In this "internal play space," we help make room for the genuine encounter, a care-filled ministry of presence, with others.

Such practice enabled one pastor to be openly responsive and interactive while praying with hospital patients.

Rev. Bonnie asked for prayer requests for the family gathered around the bedside of Matilda. As she prayed aloud, Rev. Bonnie heard the voice of another praying aloud with her. Pastor Bonnie stopped praying, and asked Matilda if she would like to pray instead. The patient said, "Oh no, Chaplain, I want you to pray for me—I just want to pray along with you." This was an interactive cultural experience of prayer that was meaningful for the patient, as well as a playfully creative rendering of this pastor's experience of prayer. Sometimes, patients teach the pastor how to play in prayer.

The practice of prayer helps to make our ears bigger and our mouths smaller. Julia Ching in a book on Chinese religions describes the image of an ancient wisdom figure; the large, bronze, millennium-old figure has very large ears, signifying the wisdom of listening.[14]

The practice of contemplative prayer helps to make our ears bigger and our mouths smaller.

Creating a Memory of Play

Building up the memory muscle of play is another helpful spiritual practice. Through cultural habit, we may develop the tendency to talk more easily about troubles than about joys. It may be difficult to hold both the pain and joy together in our lives. Fostering a playful habit of being may help those who have trouble enjoying life in spite of its incredible challenges and difficulties. As we practice playing, our bodies may develop the capacity to remember play and to seek its creative expression in various dimensions of life.

When I first started swimming, for instance, I was only able to swim a few laps before tiring. With practice, I increased the length and duration of my ability. My body now "remembers" these experiences of exercise play and indicates through agitation, tension, and restlessness when it is time again to swim. Similarly by creating a memory of play, we will remind ourselves when it is time again to play. We develop the muscle strength, or the capacity, to play only through continual practice. Through play practice, we don't necessarily put an end to problems or difficulties but we do gain strength of perspective for working with these challenges. Through play practice we infuse and reframe life — or perhaps life infuses and reframes us — so that we are paradoxically invigorated and refreshed through that which may have initially took great effort.

One purpose in cultivating a memory of play is illustrated by the insight of a pastoral counselor who specializes in work with couples.[15] In therapy with couples, the counselor begins with the necessary healing of painful dynamics and miscommunication in the relationship that have brought people to this juncture. Once this level of work is sufficiently complete, the counselor encourages couples to reflect on occasions when they experience joy together. The counselor reports that many people have trouble with this because it carries them into the realm of the unknown and the unexplored. People are not familiar with, have forgotten how, or are not accustomed to sharing joy together. It is as if their adult muscles of play have atrophied, and as a result, the relationship suffers. After the defeating patterns of negativity, hurt, betrayal, and anger recede, couples may still feel themselves in a vacuum. In spite of the desire to heal pain and miscommunication, familiarity with the terrain can pull couples back into troublesome and destructive dynamics. All prefer, at times, to remain in pain and misery simply because we are more familiar with it. Creating a memory of play is an intentional means to short-circuit the pain and negativity loop in order to make room for occasions of surprise, elation, and ecstasy. Creating a memory of play makes room for joy.

Laughter and Humor

Laughter and humor, as verbal and psychological play, are sometimes neglected but highly valuable spiritual practices. Pastoral ministers encourage and model these practices knowing that the freedom to play arises from the freedom of a God who plays.[16] We practice the classical virtue of *eutrapelia,* a combination of wit and versatility, to navigate the social middle ground between making fools of ourselves and being completely inflexible.[17] Laughter and humor, as the ancient virtue of *eutrapelia* makes clear, should not demean and dehumanize others.[18] While staying aware of the destructive side of humor and laughter, pastors and people of faith can share in the pleasure of their enlightening and energizing potential.[19] Allowing ourselves to laugh and find humor in ministry keeps us from exhaustion and reminds us not to take ourselves too seriously. We might otherwise not glimpse "God playing hide-and-seek with humanity."[20]

With laughter and humor we recognize the incongruities and inconsistencies of life.[21] Sometimes ministers just need to practice laughing with others, and in so doing give them permission to laugh freely and spontaneously. Laughter and the expression of humor are often signs that we are playing and evidence of creative resistance to narrowed vision in ourselves and others. Laughter is a misfit gift, and when shared in the spirit of Christ's inclusive care for all, is a blessed experience of our shared humanity.

> *Laughter and the expression of humor are often signs that we are playing and evidence of creative resistance to narrowed vision in ourselves and others.*

As a pastor, I once visited a generally affable parishioner who had been admitted to the intensive care unit of the regional hospital with heart problems. During our conversation, Susan said something humorous. So naturally, I laughed. My laughter sparked hers and together we were joined in an experience of joyful revelry. I know the laughter was restorative and healing for Susan because she later commented that it made her feel more "at home" even in the unfamiliar surroundings of the hospital. Yet a nurse gestured for us to be quiet, and I realized that the laughter might be a disturbance to others on the unit. Laughter and humor have pitfalls as well as exciting possibilities in playful pastoral care.

The experience highlights both a caution and an invitation when playing in pastoral care ministry. Ministers need to proceed with care since laughter is not always warranted or wanted. In this example, the environment was not entirely conducive to play. The proximity to other patients, the seriousness of physical illness, and the attitude of some healthcare professionals made for a complex situation. Regardless of the benefits, continued laughter under these circumstances would have been inappropriate. Yet when we care well for laughter and humor, these qualities enhance the experience of joy in caring relationships.

Play as embodied wisdom in ministry, and imaged as a holy fool, offers soul healing in the practices of pastoral care. Pastoral ministers, as people of faith who minister in contexts of complexity and challenge, serve as ambassadors of many gifts that reveal themselves artfully and creatively in moments of serendipitous play. Let us reclaim and celebrate play as a soulful response to God.

Questions for Personal and Group Reflection

1. Identify a person who has shown you the meaning of God's holy foolishness. What do you most admire about this person? What would it take for you to embody these characteristics?

2. How do you "play by ear" or "sculpt to discover the image" in care ministries? What supportive practices can the congregation put in place to foster playful and heart-ful care-giving and -receiving?

3. What creative adaptations have you or your community implemented to worship life or rituals of care? How have these changes made a difference for people, either positively or negatively?

4. Describe a situation of care in which humor and/or laughter was restorative to the soul. How did your attitude or that of the other person(s) contribute to the interaction?

5. Read Psalm 104 and reflect on the images of God's playful whimsy in this passage. What imaginative or concrete step in ministry does this reflection invite you to take?

6. Who and/or what makes you smile with delight? How do you welcome or dismiss such persons and occasions in times of care?

7. How do you and your congregation currently address both spiritual and real homelessness in the community? Identify care and advocacy practices that can sustain people through this experience.

8. We give and receive care in different ways depending on many circumstances, including our stage in life. Given your life stage, what distinct contributions do you make to playful ministries of care?

9. How can the principles of simplicity, loyalty, and prophecy guide creative care practices in your ministry and congregation?

10. Describe a situation when care developed in an unpredictable direction. What wisdom did you glean from the experience?

7 All I Ever Needed to Know I Learned on the Playground

Insights and Practices for Pastoral Leadership

> *Wholehearted play has the power to transform your life.*
>
> —Dainin Katagiri
> *You Have to Say Something*

Images influence the practice of ministry in powerful ways.[1] A playground offers an image of communal ministry that teaches us something about how to live from the "de-centered center"[2] in a world where clashing egos and self-aggrandizement seem to be the norm. The playground showcases the value of the community interacting with one another and de-emphasizes the function of the pastoral leader.

Playground as Metaphor for Ministry

A number of characteristics describe the playground. A playground has boundaries and lots of space: paved areas are marked with painted lines, and grassy areas offer room to run. Playgrounds are great places to romp around and fun can be had with only a few play items: balls, marbles or jacks, swings, and slides. The natural environment exposes its players to fresh air, sunlight, birds, squirrels, and other forms of life. Playgrounds engage creative imagination as the space itself draws people into interaction with one another.

Childhood lessons from the playground can inform the adult practice of ministry. We learned about:

- relating within groups;
- working constructively with conflict;
- growing in flexibility and confidence in ways that only experiencing-for-ourselves seems to allow;
- trusting ourselves as well as other people, which in turn builds confidence to try new and daring things;
- tolerating times of tension and frustration that inevitably come;
- engaging fairly;
- negotiating with appropriate words instead of hitting;
- listening to the playground monitor and coaching our peers when needed;
- returning to the classroom with other work tasks when the bell rang;
- rotating others in so that everyone had an opportunity; and
- playing for its sheer joy without keeping score of "winners" and "losers."

As adults we encounter impediments to enjoyment on the playground, including self-judgment and internal criticism as well as being ostracized or excluded by others. High expectations and perfectionism also stifle the can-do spirit that draws others in and elicits cheers and accolades. Casting oneself as a star instead of a team or cooperative player can be a hindrance.   *Ego*

The Playground in Context

The playground can be a useful metaphor for pastoral ministry if placed in context, and it includes several significant features. First, the playground is intercultural by nature; even if membership in a local church is largely comprised of one ethnic group, people likely interact with others in their neighborhoods or workplaces who are different from themselves. The playground is a setting that welcomes *play as a spiritual practice*

multicultural diversity. It provides sufficient space for flexibility and exploration, recognizing that barriers of bias and hostility limit authentic play. Second, the playground is a gathering ground for people of different generations. Pastoral ministers exercise leadership when they help people get onto the playground so that they can recognize their differences and establish common bonds. Third, contemporary playgrounds are situated within larger contexts of terrorism, war, and fear. A playground can be an image of pastoral theological resistance; in the face of fragility and uncertainty, pastors encourage practices that help harness anxiety and keep people spiritually and psychologically open to the wonder of God's creation.

Playgrounds are places of dynamic interaction that suggest important *movements* in pastoral ministry; they foster creation-centered practices that build community among people and provide space for creative self expression.

Well-Being on the Playground

The entirety of God's creation is, in a sense, intended as a playground. We are called to care for this playground because its well-being and the well-being of human beings are interconnected. Actual playgrounds and the practice of recess is in jeopardy in some places because we often erroneously assume that time should be devoted to serious subjects. The health of the playground of creation is in jeopardy as well with pollution and deforestation harming the environment. These seemingly disconnected patterns—eliminating recess and damaging the environment—reflect what Howard Clinebell calls "eco-alienation."[3] Eco-alienation is a rejection of our inherent earth-rootedness, whereas "ecobonding" is an intentional practice of claiming this relationship with the earth.[4] Eco-alienation involves two dimensions of separation—an "outer dimension," reflected in human beings' disconnection from the natural world, and an "inner dimension" that is reflected in a disconnection from our inherent wholeness as "mind-body-spirit organisms."[5]

The entirety of God's creation is, in a sense, intended as a playground. We are called to care for this playground because its well-being and the well-being of human beings are interconnected.

This internal fragmentation or eco-alienation is a faith issue because it manifests in our lives in many ways. Healing practices with the earth contribute to healing of ourselves, a practice that Clinebell calls "eco-therapy." Pastoral ministers—generalists who are not specifically trained with the same theory as psychologists, therapists, or substance-abuse counselors—can, nevertheless, influence positively the health and well-being of people by modeling eco-friendly care practices themselves and encouraging others to do the same through sound diet, exercise, and spiritual practices. They may help alleviate the stresses of life that exacerbate mental illnesses, physical obesity, and alcohol and substance abuse.

Pastoral ministers can help bring the playground indoors and lead people outdoors. Bringing the playground indoors involves incorporating the natural environment within our spaces. This can include something as simple as bringing flowers into the restrooms. I smiled when I saw a vase of flowers on the receptacles in the men's room in a local congregation. This bit of the outdoors inside the church made me deeply glad. Another example of bringing the playground indoors has to do with arranging space inside the church. Once while conducting an adult education course with a group all lined up in rows I thought we needed a change. So I asked the participants to arrange themselves in a circle, and we continued class. The movement from rows to a circle created the sense of space in the room. One participant reflected, "The give-and-take was really good here today." Partly I think this had to do with the playspace. Bringing the playground indoors also has to do with making our spaces more environmentally friendly.

- Bring the environment into your space with nature photographs on the walls.

Beauty

- Use environment-friendly cleaning products.
- Add a skylight to the building.
- Consider also the arrangements of rooms, the placement of plants and flowers, the colors of rooms, and the type of lighting.

Giving attention to these inner aesthetics can open us to the expanse of God's playground of creation.

We can go outside the playground of creation in manifold ways. Pastoral leaders can enhance the play of their congregations by engaging in season-specific outdoor activities to put us in tune with the rhythm of God's creation. In the summer, a youth group may go blackberry picking, for instance. Or a group might serve as volunteers in a shelter for homeless people during the colder months of the year. Springtime might include an all-church potluck gathering outside with the freshness of creation awakening all around in the singing of birds and the budding of trees. An autumn service project might involve members going to the homes of elderly people in the congregation or community to help prepare the yards and houses for the coming winter. These are all hands-on projects that include our moving outside to God's playground. Ecological faith practices also involve efforts that can occur in all seasons: advocacy—locally and beyond—that care for the integrity of God's creation. Sabbath-keeping becomes an ecological friendly practice that fosters well-being for ourselves and the planet as we choose options for keeping our days "green." Such practices might entail riding a bicycle instead of driving a car, sitting outside under a shade tree instead of turning on the air conditioning inside, or checking a book out from the local library instead of purchasing our own copy.

Transitions

Playgrounds are transitional spaces in which we feel ourselves more playfully present; they also provide helpful space for paying attention to and navigating through transitions. Whatever the transition may be—preparing for an impending retirement, sending children to college, discerning next steps in vocation, developing new congregational ministries — the playground image suggests three interrelated movements. Paying attention to these movements, and helping to lead people fruitfully through them, is a hallmark of playful leadership both for individuals and for communities.

- Anticipation. Anticipating transition can have an admixture of fear and anxiety as well as excitement. Playgrounds invite both fear and excitement. Young children balance playing with sheer abandon with the challenge of swinging higher and harder on the swings and climbing to the top of the tallest slide. We may look forward to play with a sense of can't-wait-to-get-there enthusiasm because we need a break from what we're doing or because we are bored. Or we might be nervous of the playground because of who we might meet or past experiences on playgrounds. Our feelings and thoughts about transitions can largely be influenced by circumstance, whether or not we have a choice in the matter, and memory of prior transitions. Even positive change — an activity that we look forward to—can trigger feelings of anxiety, and this is a normal human response. Pastoral leaders should bear in mind that going out to the playground—like moving into transition times in our individual or congregational life — is not without its accompanying feelings of excitement and fear or anxiety.

- Participation. Everyone engages differently on the playground. There is no one template for playing or moving through periods of transition. Pastoral leaders can be mindful that people and communities progress at different rates of speed. So how can we assess that people are healthfully engaged in transitions? What are signposts that help us recognize active participation? For individuals, we know that people actively participate in transition if they are willing to engage in the process or say they are experiencing movement. Active participation in transitions for some people may, at minimum, mean they do not resist change even if they cannot embrace it fully. Active engagement on the playground of transition can look very different depending on the perspective. We know that people are participating playfully in transition if they are willing to consider alternatives, ask questions, make and revise plans, and test new ideas.

- Integration. In the phase of integration, we remember the playground experience and seek ways to infuse our individual and common life with that vibrant energy. Individuals and communities grow in Christian identity as they incorporate insights and learning from the playground of transition into other areas of congregational life. Transitional or interim periods in our lives and congregations can be immensely important for maintaining health and discerning God's vision for the future.

Learning New Games

On the playground we may learn new games at our own individual pace. At every stage of life and faith, what we learn keeps our routines and habits from becoming ruts. Pastors of communities who build new challenges into their pastoral ministry offer an environment in which creativity thrives and learning occurs.

On the playground—following the practice of non-coercion—everyone can make choices to foster creativity.[6]

Positive   psychology   Risk

- *Develop what you lack.* Strengthen the creative muscle by taking initiative; overcome reluctance to try new things. Experts in the area of exercise physiology, for instance, point out that bodies get accustomed to routine, so it is important to introduce variation. In spiritual terms, disciplines of faith such as regular prayer and worship are vital to feeling connected to God. Once the routine is established, people and communities benefit from stretching themselves spiritually.

- *Shift from openness to closure.* Creative people are simultaneously open to new ideas and practices and willing to engage in hard work. Opening ourselves to the exuberant energy of the playground with all of its possibilities is followed by concentrating on one activity, such as playing one game at a time. Creativity is a synergy of open possibility and hard work.

Focus

- *Aim for complexity.* People rise to challenge through incremental and increasingly difficult steps toward complexity. Creative ministers and communities embrace the challenge of creative complexity, recognizing that Jesus the Living Christ meets us in this effort. Boredom and trivialization drag down individuals and congregations. Complexity need not diminish with age. Consider Hilda Ringe who at ninety-eight years old is engaged in her church's ministry of knitting shawls for people in need. While she is no longer able to make home care visits to others, Hilda cares for members and friends through the gift of her beautiful handiwork.

Playground Relationships and Practices

Friends, Undifferentiated Others, and Enemies

Playgrounds are spaces where relationships are formed and developed. But not all of the relationships are of the same depth. On the playground, we encounter friends, enemies, and the large group of undifferentiated others who are neither. As pastoral leaders, we encounter different layers of relationships within our congregations and are responsible for helping others navigate these relationships within community. In the rest of this chapter, we explore the different kinds of relationships that comprise play on the playground: friends, undifferentiated others, and enemies or those we want to ignore. We are mostly accustomed to *playing with our friends, steering clear of our enemies, and ignoring the others.* Jesus invites us, as he did all of the disciples into a new form of relationship: "no longer do I call you disciples, but friends." Pastoral leaders tend to playground practices in ministry to help communities live into the friendship of God.

Fostering a Society of Friends on the Playground

An exegesis of John 15:12-17 offers insights for grounding friendship in a Christian context. In this passage, Jesus invites the disciples into a new kind of relationship in the form of a commandment, taking love as its operative principle. As Gail O'Day points out, the word

Open space for be-friending

"friend" in vv. 13-15 is from the Greek *phileo* (to love).[7] John's gospel uses two Greek verbs (*agape* and *phileo*) interchangeably. When Jesus uses the word "friend," the reference is to "those who are loved."[8] It is not a friendship based on utility or pleasure (the first two Aristotlean notions), but mutual reciprocity, deep caring, and regard. Such love comes from the depths; we might call it transformational love. Sharon Ringe suggests that "Jesus is the lover/friend whose love affects life in the beloved by granting them an intimacy with God that itself can be called friendship with God."[9] Out of the depths of his relationship in God, Jesus invites us into relationship without secrets. In the mutual intimacy of such friendship, Jesus shares with the beloved companions everything that has been made known to him. Through the call to friendship, Jesus is reshaping the presumed order of the Master/disciple relationship, and by so doing issues a call that we love and befriend one another. The playground is both an imagined and real place for the great meeting of friends.

> *When Jesus uses the word "friend," it is not a friendship based on utility or pleasure, but mutual reciprocity, deep caring, and regard. Such love comes from the depths; we might call it transformational love.*

The playground does not exist only as an actual place of play, but also an *internal playground* where we encounter the living God in our own souls. The Sufi poet Rumi reflects, "Out beyond ideas of right doing and wrong doing, there is a field. I'll meet you there."[10] Notice the language, out beyond *ideas* is a meeting place. This "field" is an internal space not governed by preconceived notions, rules, standards, or family or cultural expectations. Difficult to capture in words, this field is essentially a state of awareness, or what Brother Lawrence once called "practicing the presence of God."[11]

Dualistic thinking prematurely differentiates between this and that, self and other, wrong and right, thus limiting creative possibilities. Rumi's field of meeting is like an "inner playground," a capacity within each of us to encounter the truth and joy of our very being. We long to know the Holy who dwells in this "inner field" beyond right and wrong. Once we find this field, through intention or stumbling, we want to linger there to know, as the mystics of every age and Julian of Norwich in particular have echoed: all will be well, and every kind of thing will be well.[12]

God dwells within us on this "inner playground," the birthplace of the Holy Spirit, the temple of the Holy within. *The inner playground is the sacred sanctuary where the Holy plays within us.* We attend to this place because it is here where a new and mysterious thing can happen: it is here where the possible is born out of the seemingly impossible. We are not the creators of the playground, but we are most assuredly called to become the caretakers of the inner space for holy play.

The image of the inner playground suggests a free space or what some have called "the void" in the human psyche.[13] We might be used to calling the playground by another name, such as the void, emptiness, inner lack, or hole. When we encounter this space, we have a tendency to want to fill it with busyness, thoughts, plans, or even alcohol and drugs. This holy playground of God is intended for a different purpose: to be free for God's creative and playful work. Filling this space ourselves does not leave it free for the work of the Divine within us.

FREE   FOR   ★

Friends as Coaches on the Playground

The role of pastoral leader entails cultivation of a company of friends within a community, peers who can teach and coach one another. So pastors can be effective by developing programs within the congregation in order sometimes to get out of the way, as it were, so that people can fulfill this ministry. Playful pastoral leaders encourage the building up of the community of coaches and coaching practices.[14]

All of us need companions on the spiritual journey. Support and encouragement comes from those who may have experience or ability within range of our own. Pastoral leaders provide effective guidance when they support and encourage companionship among peers, something I call spiritual coaching. Coaching is valuable for such practices as prayer life, service in the community, child rearing, moving into retirement, caring for aging family members, and so forth. In my view, peer coaching can relate to any sphere of our lives because God calls us to well-being and intends us to live balanced lives.

The following are a few playground guidelines for spiritual coaching:

- Choose a trustworthy guide—a person or small group of people who have insight or experience in an area of growth or challenge. A trustworthy guide is someone to whom you can tell the truth without fear of scorn or belittlement.

- Sort and establish specific priorities. Identify an area or practice you would like to develop. Perhaps life circumstance has provided an urgent situation—the need to lose weight because of a health crisis, for example.

- Set measurable goals. If the priority is to lose weight, then the next step is to determine how much and in what time period.

- Build in times for celebration. As a way to recognize hard work or commitment, find way to rejoice in meeting goals or commitments.

- Evaluate the process. Check in regularly with the coach throughout the process. Determine when and how long to consult—maybe short conversations by phone once a week is sufficient; if the coach is a group, a set time of an hour once a week or every other week might be best.

- Maintain. Keep up the commitment to the new practice (or mission) and integrate others. For individuals—check in periodically with the coaching companion; for groups—consider ways to continue faithfully with the ministry.

The process is meant to be collaborative and mutual as the company of friends becomes coaches for one another, sharing the gifts of God in community.

Play practice as spiritual coaching builds on the assumption that we are called into community as the friends of God to build up God's community and are meant to enlarge the circle. Playing is an act of hospitality in which we open ourselves to engage and welcome the other.[15] It is an act of trust that enlarges each participant. Playing together with friends is delightful and allows for healthy competition, ✝ encouragement to try out new things with a group cheering us on, the freedom to say yes or no, and to sit on the sideline. In God's community, we can trust that is it sufficient to be ourselves.

In God's community, we can trust that is it sufficient to be ourselves.   You are Enough.

On the playground among friends, we enter the internal gateway to the creative imagination, a source of God's hope for the church. We can daydream as we let our minds roam free. We open ourselves to the wonder and awe that comes from releasing our many preoccupations so that God can dream a dream within us.

Learning to Talk to the Undifferentiated "Others"

Playgrounds may contain people that we don't even notice. Maybe we are becoming aware of these others on the playground and want to become better acquainted, to take the initiative toward friendship. Let's consider the case of playing on the interfaith playground—without conflict—as a situation in which we want to learn about those many others on the playground. Perhaps our community has noticed an influx of people of a different denomination or religious faith background; perhaps we have a congregation in which there are interfaith families. Such is the case of a Protestant congregation in Columbia, Maryland (Columbia United Christian Church) with several Christian-Jewish couples in the community. Faith traditions meet one another in many ways.

- Designated representatives may gather to craft a document of mutual interest.
- Meetings may occur in the lives of individual and group members of those traditions.

- We often come to know one another through intentional conversation or dialogue.

Playgrounds create the emotional space and physical possibility for dialogue. We can choose to talk with one another by establishing the conditions that seem appropriate for everyone involved. The playground also has limits for genuine dialogue; those who have been harmed, wounded, or outcast may be reluctant or unwilling to engage within this space. On the playground, we generally have breathing room for interaction that is open-hearted and open-minded, thus increasing the likelihood for "mutual transformation" of faith perspectives among participants.[16] The transformational quality of dialogue occurs within and beyond the actual encounter with the other.

Authentic dialogue, expressed in words and embodied in presence with one another, involves risk and has two phases "beyond" the exchange of words and ideas: 1) crossing over and returning back, and 2) witnessing to the truths in one's faith tradition. This model establishes the conditions for everyone's faith to be informed and transformed.[17] Developed as a means for Buddhist-Christian dialogue, this model offers a means for genuine encounter in other dimensions of faith as well.

The first phase of the dialogue involves two movements: crossing over and returning back. When we listen to another in a posture of alive and open awareness we learn something about the other's story, history, and faith. We therefore *cross over* to learn about the faith experience of the other and to know more about the other. In this movement, we are educating ourselves. Our open listening to the faith and tradition of the other may give us insights or wisdom that have been undervalued or excluded from our own experience and tradition. So, we *return back* to our traditions, our denominations, families, and congregations to examine whether and how to "restructure our heritage in the light of what we have learned."[18]   *Cross-pollination*

The second phase involves sharing our truth with the other. The goal of witnessing, in Cobb's view, is "to lead the other to attend to what we believe to be the truth and to be transformed by it."[19] We acknowledge the weaknesses and "repent of the atrocities" of our traditions, while sharing the truth as we have encountered it and believe it to be helpful to the other. This mutual sharing of truth through story is evangelism, beyond the "recitation of set formulae."[20] Cobb's language about sharing truth with the intention of transforming the other indicates a sense of control or manipulation. My sense is that truth does not require persuasion. It speaks for itself and people can choose to recognize it or not. We come to recognize the validity of truth in whatever time is needed. Mutual transformation describes open-hearted and open-minded sharing without coercion: We share awareness of truth and then release control of the outcome, trusting that the Truth itself will set us free, to echo the language of John's gospel. Such are the dynamics of dialogue on a playground.

Dialogue involves more than a theoretical encounter between people. In the process of dialogue, that which was undifferentiated and diffuse about the other will come into direct focus. We may or may not like what we encounter. Genuine dialogue, according to Denise Dombkowski Hopkins, occurs when we move beyond the stage of simply being nice to one another and touch pushpoints of pain.[21] *ouch* ★

The benefit to dialogue or conversation is that we get to know one another and keep lines of communication open, allowing for friendly relations even if we would not exactly call ourselves friends. Conversation with these many others, our neighbors, reduces the expression of negative playground attributes such as unhealthy competition or conflict, keeping score, or holding grudges with the intention of "getting even." Learning to see the image of God in the many undifferentiated others is a mark of spiritual growth and maturity. Conversation with one another across faith communities and denominations brings us to recognize that God's playground is much more expansive than our own.

Dialogue, or conversation, also shifts our preconceived notions of winning and losing. The eastern principle of yin-yang, which emerges from a worldview that values harmony and harmonious social relationships, is helpful because it helps us to see that within each experience of winning, there is also one of losing; and within each loss is a win.

The challenge in our winning and our losing is the ability to hold the other possibilities in our perspective. Humility involves this recognition; we do not deny the winning or success, but its attainment is grounded by the realization that other results are also possible. Such humility can be fruitfully learned on the playground.

Loving the Enemy: Recognizing the Bullies

The playground as a metaphor for ministry provides ground for difficult practices as well. Though it's not necessarily an easy subject to acknowledge, especially in religious settings, we have to interact constructively with our enemies. On the playground, enemies are usually bullies, and bullying can come in many forms and degrees of behavior, including:

- accusative and blaming language,
- predatory action,
- monopolizing behavior in conversations,
- pressuring tactics,
- purposefully hiding information, or
- threatening harm.

The bullies can be members of the congregation and/or the larger community. Instead of trying to deny the presence of bullies, communities can establish practices that help protect people from becoming the victims of such actions.

What we teach our children we need to learn to do ourselves. On the playground, a monitor can help children relate constructively to bullying behavior. As adults we are often left to make these judgments for ourselves. We can, however, become advocates within our organizations. Two specific practices help with bullying on the playground: backing away and returning with friends. Stepping back allows for the gathering of thoughts and the calming of emotions, thus interrupting the cycle. Parents teach children to do this by encouraging a period of "time out." Adults need this practice as well; we can be models or teachers for others by taking the opportunity to step back and take the time to reflect.

The second practice is to return with friends. On the playground it can be dangerous to confront bullying behavior by one's self, so it is important to have watchful friends around to help monitor behavior. This communal practice keeps the potentially harmful tactics of the bully contained. Bullies may antagonize one person, but they cannot take on a whole group; in the face of such opposition, the bully is likely to retreat or behave. "Return with friends" is another way of reminding us to return to a seemingly unwinnable or losing situation with additional resources. The resources may include:

- consulting with trusted others about tactical and logistical problems,

- changing in attitude or perspective about a particular scenario such as reframing a situation, or

- finding support for what you are doing since sometimes going it alone creates confusion.

Anger and Play

Anger gets sparked on the playground. Anger can be a difficult emotion for many religious people. It can feel like a bomb going off inside of us, an explosion usually triggered by recent or old memories. Anger's physical sensations may include mild irritation, an internal firestorm, boiling pot, headache, or tension. Internalized messages from our early childhood as well conditioned religious messages both conscious and unconscious influence the ability to work with anger.[22]

The playground makes space for two dominant tendencies with anger, *the avoiders* and *the exploders*,[23] to at least attempt to play together. Many things happen on the playground as we step on each other's toes, forget to take turns, insist on doing it our way, or feel attacked by an on-coming ball. Allowing for more space with anger reflects the to-and-fro movement of play itself. We can experience both the so-called up feelings of exhilaration, joy, thrill, and excitement as

temporary nature

well as the so-called down feelings of hurt, rejection, and disappointment. We experience many emotions on the playground, none of which
is permanent. Imagining ourselves working with anger on the playground gives us permission to experience the often intense and unsettling feelings as a way to explore what is occurring.

Carroll Saussy, pastoral counselor and theologian, identifies a three-
part discernment process for relating with anger. Ultimately, she calls
religious people to "befriend" anger as way to harness its energy for
faithful action in God's world. Saussy writes, "Befriend your anger.
Learn to stay with it, to play with it, to leap back to its roots. There
you'll find a child in fear and pain . . . return, an adult with compassion."[24] The playground offers a testing ground for the practice of be-
friending anger. Some people were fortunate enough to have watchful
mentors, pastors, teachers, and coaches who encouraged us to "stay
in the game" even through frustration, a milder form of anger. These
same people also helped to negotiate difficulties between people or
stop a fight when it had ensued. As "watchful and trusting" others,
they helped make us feel safe and secure so that we could learn with
others and then play with abandon. Referees helped negotiate dynamics at the emotional flashpoints that usually involved conflictual anger
as well as crying, yelling, and sulking. If we were lucky we had these
people with us on the playground so that we could "internalize" the
lessons we learned and make them our own. Eventually, we no longer
needed the mentor or teacher to watch out for us because we could do
this for ourselves.

Playing on the playground with anger has a few movements that
we need to attend to as people of faith and religious leaders. Saussy
calls this a "Model for Dealing with Anger."[25] The steps in this model,
in my view, are movements of energy that we can discern within and
among us:

1. **Hear the call:** spend time with your experience of anger in order to
   understand yourself and the situation at hand.

2. **Discern God's lure:** determine whether this is a *call to action* or a *call to
   surrender.*

3. **Strategize your response:** plan, act, evaluate; if you choose to surrender your anger, then determine whether you need to do anything else to bring closure to the experience.

We don't usually think of anger as something to play with since the energy often seems antithetical to play. When we don't pay attention to and learn from our outbursts of anger, though, we ultimately hurt ourselves and others. Pastoral ministers can help communities as they themselves are willing to model and teach others to devote loving attention to anger.

Anger to Serendipitous Embrace

The playground, as an arena for play and enjoyment, can also become a place of tension and conflict that intentionally excludes people from participation. Whether intentional or accidental, exclusions hurt everyone because such action tears at the fabric of community. God calls us, within the space of creative freedom, to reach toward one another.

Miroslav Volf develops the theological basis for reaching out to embrace those who make us angry or those we would most like to avoid.[26] Written in response to the heinous and exclusionary practices of regimes and organizations in the twentieth century, Volf proposes that a Christian response to exclusion is the practice of embrace.[27] In living practice, the embrace of the other person or community can be enormously difficult because of the anger and pain already separating people. The practice of embrace, in my view, is not a commandment, but a gift of grace. Embrace is a practice that individual Christians and communities work toward, with awareness that full reconciliation is a gift of the Holy Spirit. Exclusionary behavior spans a continuum from seemingly minor incidents to large-scale obliteration of members of the human family.[28] Communities need to implement safeguards to protect people from exclusion, such as rules for hiring practices and employment. Embrace means that we do not ignore, sanction, or permit exclusionary behavior.

The practice of embrace, expanding the circle on the playground to include more and more players, reflects my view of a welcoming, inclusive God who embraces all of humanity. Pastoral ministry is about welcoming and including people into the household of God. As welcoming people, we reflect God's hospitality as expressed in Jesus Christ and ritualized in the communion meal: an act in which we mirror the Holy "making-space-for-us-and-inviting-us-in."[29] Pastoral ministry on the playground moves toward inclusion and embrace wherever possible.

An embrace is comprised several smaller gestures, each varying in duration: opening the arms, waiting, closing the arms in the actual embrace; and opening the arms again.[30] The heart of the embrace is the actual moment of reciprocal connection with another body-person, and each of the other components of the encounter are valuable for helping to heal the tension and division of conflict. Any effort we can make toward embracing "the other" in our faith communities contributes to the healing of the whole. An embrace is a physical moment of connection that expresses in bodily form the words: "God values you." We let the embrace go from our arms, entrusting the other person to the loving arms of God. An embrace is also an act of faith because there is no guarantee of what will follow, although we can be assured that one or both parties will be changed in some way. With arms outstretched, we wait for an embrace that might never be reciprocated; this can be a fragile, tender, and emotionally laden experience.

On the fluid and imaginative setting of the playground, though, the gestures themselves are often jumbled. The playground reorders the predictable so that in a flash we might even spontaneously hug an "enemy" and only later come to realize what we've just done. Such shocking reorganization is what play has the potential to do for our psyches, souls, and communities. Some might say that it's all imaginary and simply child's play. We wonder how such possibilities could ever become reality. No one knows for sure, but isn't it worth a playful attempt?

Following the Call

In pastoral theological practice, I hope, for ourselves and our parishioners, we all find space for this much needed exploration because the question of what it means to be human together is Christ's invitation to us. The playground as a "good-enough" image illumines some of the vital practices of pastoral ministry. This image is a place of new beginnings where God sparks our imaginations and renews our energy. Playgrounds exist in relationship to a larger environment; a playground, while integral to the whole, is only part of the ecology necessary for a vital ministry. The playground as a misfit image for ministerial leadership is a field of creative and serendipitous imperfection where, surrounded by the company of others, we respond to God's call to play.

Questions for Personal and Group Reflection

1. How does the image of a playground shift your understanding of what can occur in a context of ministry?

2. What season of the year best captures your stage in life? In ministry? What opportunities for play await in this season?

3. What play practices can be introduced or developed in your congregation to foster a society of holy friendship?

4. Identify a person in your life who could serve as spiritual coach. Develop a covenant for the coaching relationship with one or two play goals you would like to achieve.

5. Consider the situations on the playground that are most likely to provoke your anger. How might you befriend your own anger as well as the other people toward whom you might direct that anger?

6. Reflect on playground experiences in your history. What makes you enthusiastic and/or hesitant about the playground as an image for ministry?

7. Genuine dialogue takes initiative and effort. How might play be incorporated into your community's times of conversation?

8. Name your favorite playground apparatuses. How can *this kind* of experience of play be captured in ministry?

9. What ethical guidelines has your community implemented to protect people from bullying behavior? If practices are not in place, consider steps for action.

10. How does your congregation foster faithful Sabbath-keeping? Identify personal and communal ways of making Sabbath days "green."

Notes

Chapter One: Playfully Misfit

1. I borrow this definition from Kathleen J. Greider, *Reckoning with Aggression* (Louisville: Westminster/John Knox, 1997), 9.

2. Jung Young Lee, *Marginality: The Key to Multicultural Theology* (Minneapolis: Fortress Press, 1995), 7.

3. Barbara Wheeler writes, "The marginal status of organized religion is very likely the basic cause of the difficulty attracting leaders for religious organizations. People of ability, especially the young, seek social roles that position them to make a substantial difference. The internal weakness of many religious organizations and their lack of influence in the wider society limit the amount of impact their leaders can expect to have." "Fit for Ministry?" *Christian Century* (April 22, 2001): 23.

4. Matthew Fox suggests some of the values listed here. See *The Reinvention of Work* (San Francisco: HarperSanFrancisco, 1994).

5. My own working definition of play builds on the hypothesis that the phenomenon cannot be completely captured in words. See also Johan Huizinga, *Homo Ludens: A Study of the Play Element in Culture* (Boston: Beacon, 1955).

6. James Dittes, *Re-Calling Ministry* (St. Louis: Chalice, 1999), 182. Emphasis added.

7. As a master metaphor, play is sufficiently multifaceted to elucidate complex and ambiguous experience. See Brian Sutton-Smith, *The Ambiguity of Play* (Cambridge, Mass.: Harvard University Press, 1997).

8. Among a number of publications on professional ethics and the ministry, I recommend the following: Gaylord Noyce, *Pastoral Ethics: Professional Responsibilities of the Clergy* (Nashville: Abingdon, 1988); and Karen Lebacqz and Joseph D. Driskill, *Ethics and Spiritual Care: A Guide for Pastors, Chaplains, and Spiritual Directors* (Nashville: Abingdon, 2000).

9. Page Smith, *Killing the Spirit* (New York: Viking, 1990), 205.

Chapter Two: Play and Grief

1. Winnicott calls this the potential or intermediate space. See D. W. Winnicott, *Playing and Reality* (New York: Basic Books, 1971), 110.

2. Psychological dynamics and theological implications of grieving are explored further in two useful resources: Kenneth R. Mitchell and Herbert Anderson, *All Our Losses, All Our Griefs* (Louisville: Westminster John Knox, 1983); and Roslyn A. Karaban, *Complicated Losses, Difficult Deaths* (San Jose, Calif.: Resource Publications, 2000).

3. Laurent A. Parks Daloz, Cheryl H. Keen, James P. Keen, Sharon Daloz Parks, *Common Fire* (Boston: Beacon, 1996), 63.

4. Ibid., 72.

5. Ibid.

6. Ibid., 73.

7. Kathleen Greider, *Reckoning with Aggression* (Louisville: Westminster John Knox, 1997), 9.

8. Ann Ulanov and Barry Ulanov, *Religion and the Unconscious* (Philadelphia: Westminster, 1975), 95.

9. In fact, Jack Katz, a social psychologist at University of California, Los Angeles, argues against the widely held perspective that considers emotions "as opposed to thinking." Jack Katz, *How Emotions Work* (Chicago: University of Chicago Press, 1999), 7.

10. I argue that grief is a significant and largely unexamined emotion for misfit leaders and congregations. Jung Young Lee identifies other emotional aspects of marginalization, including rejection, humiliation, alienation, loneliness, nothingness, wholeness and a new type of new life. See *Marginality: The Key to Multicultural Theology* (Minneapolis: Fortress, 1995), 162–170.

11. Greider, *Reckoning with Aggression*, 48–55.

12. Daniel Goleman's work helps us see, in more detail, the complex processes by which the brain "reads" emotions before the rational part of the brain is "aware" of what is taking place. Goleman argues that intellectual intelligence alone does not offer persons preparation for the challenges that life inevitably brings. The development of emotional intelligence, or what others have called character, can offer a means for navigating these challenges. Goleman contends that "emotional aptitude is a *meta-ability*" that governs how well persons employ the skills they have, including rational intelligence. *Emotional Intelligence* (New York: Bantam, 1996), 43. The connections between emotions and leadership practices is developed in Daniel Goleman et al., *Primal Leadership: Learning to Lead with Emotional Intelligence* (Cambridge: Harvard Business School Press, 2004).

13. David W. Augsburger defines this term as "an intentional cognitive envisioning and affective experiencing of another's thoughts and feelings, even though the thoughts rise from another process of knowing, the values grow from another frame of moral reasoning, and the feelings spring from another basis of assumptions." *Pastoral Counseling across Cultures* (Philadelphia: Westminster, 1986), 29.

14. I view grief as a life-long process, ranging from acute to barely noticeable through which we attend to experiences of loss and pain, both large and small. A number of scholarly practitioners have attended to the various "stages" of grieving and loss. For elaborated discussion of different stage theories, see Yorick Spiegel, *The Grief Process,* trans. Elsbeth Duke (Nashville: Abingdon, 1977); and Elisabeth Kubler-Ross, *On Death and Dying* (New York: Macmillan, 1969).

15. John 20:11-18.

16. A helpful and expansive discussion about shame and care can be found in the following: Gershen Kaufman, *Shame: The Power of Caring,* 3rd Rev. Exp. Ed. (Cambridge: Schenkman Books, 1992).

17. Robert H. Kamm, *The Superman Syndrome: Why the Information Age Threatens Your Future and What You Can Do about It* (San Luis Obispo, Calif.: 1stBooks, 2000), 221.

18. This insight builds on the view that trust is foundational for personal and community development. See Erik H. Erikson, *Identity and the Life Cycle* (New York: W.W. Norton and Co., 1994).

19. Winnicott suggests that the role of the analyst is to foster a space in the therapeutic encounter so that persons may find or recreate a sense of self-experience that may have been lost. D.W. Winnicott, *Holding and Interpretation: Fragment of an Analysis* (New York: Grove, 1986), 7, 11, 15, 17. Cited by Ann Ulanov, *Finding Space* (Louisville: Westminster John Knox, 2001), 125.

20. Ann Ulanov, *Finding Space,* 125.

21. Ibid., 133. Ulanov argues that the "presence of self-experience conveys what Winnicott calls primary creativity."

22. Craig Dykstra, "The Pastoral Imagination," *Initiatives in Religion* 9 (Spring 2001), 1–2, 15.

23. Margaret J. Wheatley, *Leadership and the New Science* (San Francisco: Berrett-Koehler, 1992), 78.

Chapter Three: Plays and Playing

1. Quotes from Harvard Magazine, http://harvardmagazine.com/2006/05/love-in-the-last-act.html, and refer to the book by Elinor Fuchs, *Making an Exit: A Mother-Daughter Drama with Alzheimer's, Machine Tools, and Laughter* (New York: Owl, 2006).

2. Two useful resources for using drama skills to enhance learning and storytelling include: Richard W. Swanson, *Provoking the Gospel: Methods to Embody Biblical Storytelling through Drama* (Cleveland: Pilgrim, 2004); and Victoria Rue, *Theatre as Pedagogy in Religious Studies* (Cleveland: Pilgrim, 2005).

3. For explication of the theories and theorists associated with the object relations theory, see Peter Buckley M.D., ed., *Essential Papers on Object Relations* (New York: New York University Press, 1986).

Carolyn
Myss

4. For further reading about personal, family, and ministry myths, see Edward P. Wimberly, *Recalling Our Own Stories: Spiritual Renewal for Religious Caregivers* (San Francisco: Jossey-Bass, 1997).

5. An accessible volume for reflection on Jungian archetypes is Carol S. Pearson, *The Hero Within,* 3rd ed. (New York: HarperOne, 1998).

6. The following are resources for learning about characters in the Bible through our personal story: Sadie Gregory, *A New Dimension in Old Testament Story* (San Francisco: Guild for Psychological Studies, 1980); and Peter Pitzele, *Scripture Windows: Toward a Practice of Bibliodrama* (Los Angeles: Alef Design Group, 1998).

7. Ann and Barry Ulanov, *The Healing Imagination* (Einsiedeln, Switzerland: Daimon Verlag, 1999). The authors use the terms *fantasy* and *imagination* interchangeably and point to important distinguishing characteristics.

8. The following books by Augusto Boal are resources for using drama in service of social transformation: *Theatre of the Oppressed,* 3rd rev. ed. (London: Pluto Press, 2000); and *Games for Actors and Non-Actors,* 2nd ed. (New York: Routledge, 2002). For more information about the work of a creative drama group, see http://www.lookingforlilith.org.

9. For D.W. Winnicott, the true self is associated with spontaneity and creativity while the false self is associated with compliance and protection. These complementary aspects of selfhood, when in balance, are both necessary for vital functioning. See *Playing and Reality* (New York: Basic, 1971), 54; and *The Maturational Processes and the Facilitating Environment* (New York: International University Press, 1965), 147.

10. D.W. Winnicott, *Maturational Processes,* 70.

11. Ibid.

12. Helpful warm-up exercises for play readings and enactments can be found in Viola Spolin, *Theater Games for Rehearsal: A Director's Handbook* (Evanston, Ill.: Northwestern University Press, 1985).

13. Fredericka Berger acknowledges the influence of Peter Brook, *The Empty Space* (New York: Atheneum, 1968).

Chapter Four: Playful Teaching and Learning

1. Robert K. Johnston, a theologian in the evangelical tradition, argues for what he calls the recovery of a biblically based understanding of play in *The Christian at Play* (Grand Rapids: Eerdmans, 1983), 53–81. Johnston argues that play is not itself religion, but prepares the way for an experience of authentic faith. He proposes a biblical model of play using analysis of scriptural texts from the Old and New Testaments to evidence the many ways in which the Bible supports play (83–124).

2. Harvey Cox, a systematic theologian, has addressed the need to recover the value of festivity and fantasy in religious life. Cox explores the meaning of the "Feast of Fools," a holiday in medieval Europe, during which it was the custom to ridicule

Holy Hilarity Sun. following Easter

social customs and conventions. What needs to be retrieved in Western Christianity, Cox argues, is the spirit of the feast of fools, since this "spirit" of celebration and festivity can serve as a critique to social and theological notions that emphasize work and productivity as the chief purpose of humanity. In this work, based in a theological anthropology of hope, Cox also examines the experience of faith itself as a form of play. (*Feast of Fools* [Cambridge, Mass.: Harvard University Press, 1969]).

3. James E. Dittes, *Pastoral Counseling: The Basics* (Louisville: Westminster John Knox, 1999), 81–98.

4. See particularly, Sigmund Freud, *Psychopathology of Everyday Life* (New York: Macmillan, 1915), 80–114.

5. The phrase is my adaptation of a bell hooks' phrase. See her *Teaching to Transgress* (New York: Routledge, 1994).

6. Hooks's precise statement follows: "The idea that learning should be exciting, even 'fun,' was the subject of critical discussion by educators writing about pedagogical practices in grade schools, and sometimes even high schools. But there seemed to be no interest among either traditional or radical educators in discussing the role of excitement in higher education." Ibid., 7.

7. Rita Nakashima Brock, *Journeys by Heart* (New York: Crossroad, 1988), 26.

8. Ibid., 193.

9. For an extended treatment on this topic, see Marie M. Fortune, *Is Nothing Sacred?* (San Francisco: Harper and Row, 1989).

10. A number of resources exist for interpreting this personality tool. The following are recommended: David Daniels and Virginia Price, *The Essential Enneagram* (San Francisco: HarperSanFrancisco, 2000); and Renee Baron and Elizabeth Wagele, *The Enneagram Made Easy* (San Francisco: HarperSanFrancisco, 1994).

11. For a useful theoretical and practical guide to sandplay, see Rie Rogers Mitchell and Harriet S. Friedman, *Sandplay* (London: Routledge, 1994), and http://www.sandplay.org/index.htm.

Chapter Five: Leadership as Creative Adventure

1. Robert L. Kinast, *Let Ministry Teach* (Collegeville, Minn.: Liturgical, 1996), 180.

2. Oliver Wendell Holmes, cited in James W. Fowler, *Faithful Change* (Nashville: Abingdon, 1996), 177.

3. Other scholars have attended to the theological grounding for pastoral leadership. For instance, Jackson Carroll's work develops an ecclesiology for ministry in which he identifies "normative assumptions" that guide religious leaders. First, the church as the body of Christ is defined in "character and calling" by the life, death, and resurrection of Jesus Christ. A second assumption is that the church "functions as a community of meaning, belonging, and empowerment." A third assumption is that the work of ministry is a form of service to which God calls all people, both

clergy and laity. A fourth assumption is that shared ministry—among clergy and laity—does not "imply a sameness of functions." And finally, Carroll proposes that shared ministry among clergy and laity contributes to, rather than distracts from, strong leadership. Jackson W. Carroll, *As One with Authority* (Louisville: Westminster/John Knox, 1991), 79–96.

4. An elaboration on fostering beneficial change can be found in a number of church leadership resources: Scott Cormode, *Making Spiritual Sense: Christian Leaders as Spiritual Interpreters* (Nashville: Abingdon, 2006); Lewis A. Parks and Bruce C. Birch, *Ducking Spears, Dancing Madly: A Biblical Model of Church Leadership* (Nashville: Abingdon, 2004); and Lovett H. Weems, Jr., *Take the Next Step: Leading Lasting Change in the Church* (Nashville: Abingdon, 2003).

5. Bernard M. Loomer, "S-I-Z-E is the Measure," in *Religious Experience and Process Theology*, ed. Harry James Cargas and Bernard Lee (New York: Paulist, 1976), 69–76.

6. Ibid., 70.

7. Process metaphysics emphasizes that the future holds boundless possibilities for creation action, but the weight of the conditioned past influences our habitual choices toward more of the same. See Alfred North Whitehead, *Process and Reality: An Essay in Cosmology* (New York: Harper, 1960).

8. One helpful resource for dream work is Kelly Bulkeley, *Dreams of Healing: Transforming Nightmares into Visions of Hope* (Mahwah, N.J.: Paulist Press, 2003).

9. James MacGregor Burns, a prominent scholar on leadership theory, first made the distinction between transactional and transforming leadership. Transactional leadership exchanges "one thing for another" while transformational leadership "occurs when one or more persons engage with others in such a way that leaders and followers raise one another to higher levels of motivation and morality." *Leadership* (New York: Harper & Row, 1978), 4.

10. See esp. Fowler, *Faithful Change,* 177.

11. Howard Gardner's groundbreaking work, *Frames of Mind: The Theory of Multiple Intelligences* (New York: Basic, 1983) names different types of human intelligence. Gardner's more recent work expands on this generative theory: *Intelligence Reframed: Multiple Intelligences for the 21st Century* (New York: Basic Books, 2000) and *Five Minds for the Future* (Cambridge, Mass.: Harvard Business School, 2007). These resources ought to stimulate multiple ways of envisioning effective church leadership models.

12. Frederick Buechner, *Wishful Thinking: A Theological ABC* (New York: Harper & Row, 1973), 95.

13. Ibid., 20.

14. Bernard M. Loomer, "Two Kinds of Power," *Criterion* 15 (Winter 1976): 14.

15. See development of the servant leadership model in the following: Robert K.

Greenleaf, *Servant Leadership: A Journey into the Nature of Legitimate Power and Greatness* (New York: Paulist Press, 1977); and Robert K. Greenleaf et al., *Servant-Leader Within: A Transformative Path* (New York: Paulist Press, 2003).

16. Gordon D. Kaufman, "On Thinking of God as Serendipitous Creativity," *Journal of the American Academy of Religion* 69 (June 2001): 409–25.

17. Ibid., 423.

18. Ronald Heifetz, *Leadership without Easy Answers* (Cambridge: Belknap Press of Harvard University Press), 20.

19. Brian Sutton-Smith, *The Ambiguity of Play* (Cambridge: Harvard University Press, 1997), 221.

20. Ibid., 229.

21. Heifetz, *Leadership without Easy Answers*, 128.

22. Ibid., 128–29.

23. Winnicott, *Maturational Processes*, 145.

24. Jackson W. Carroll, *As One with Authority: Reflective Leadership in Ministry* (Louisville: Westminster/John Knox Press, 1991), 102.

25. See Herbert Anderson and Edward Foley, *Mighty Stories, Dangerous Rituals* (San Francisco: Jossey-Bass, 1998).

26. Elaine Ramshaw, *Ritual and Pastoral Care* (Philadelphia: Fortress Press, 1987), 88.

27. Ritual helps to hold the tension inherent in liminality, the state of living in-between roles or stages of life, and also foster what Victor Turner calls *communitas*, an egalitarian and nonhierarchical form of interpersonal and group relations. Turner, *Ritual Process* (Chicago: Aldine, 1969), 96–97.

28. See Parks et al., *Common Fire* (Boston: Beacon, 1997), 38. The authors suggest that "a good pilgrimage leads to discovery and transformation, but isn't complete until you have returned home and told your story."

29. Gadamer, *Truth and Method*, trans. Joel Weinsheimer and Donald G. Marshall, 2nd ed., (New York: Crossroad Publishing, 1989), 103.

30. Robert Sternberg and Todd Lubart point out that the "impetus toward innovation ultimately has to come from within. . . . [T]he most creative work in any field is unlikely to come from attempts to be a crowd pleaser. One needs to think in ways that others simply may not like or understand, or to ask questions that others will find *impertinent* or *irrelevant*" (emphasis added). See *Defying the Crowd* (New York: Free, 1995), 63.

31. Howard Stone suggests the helpful terminology of pastoral conversation by which he refers to a ministerial "style of purposeful interaction with parishioners" that may be employed in a formal counseling session, or in many other informal contexts that ministry provides. See, for example, "The Congregational Setting of Pastoral

Counseling: A Study of Pastoral Counseling Theorists from 1949–1999," *Journal of Pastoral Care* 55 (Summer 2001): 188.

32. Anne Streaty Wimberly, "Creating Time," *Circuit Rider* (January/February 2002): 16–17.

33. Anne Streaty Wimberly, plenary address given at the Society for Pastoral Theology Annual Study Conference, 15 June 2001.

34. Personal communication with interviewee, 18 June 2001.

35. Mihalyi Csikszentmihalyi's statement during a lecture for the course "Creativity and Innovation," Drucker School of Management, Claremont Graduate University, Claremont, Calif., Spring 2001.

36. Craig Dykstra contends that one of the elements that is important for "success" in the ministry is the development of what he calls an "internal gyroscope" or "pastoral imagination." Dykstra suggests that a pastoral imagination is a "particular way of seeing and interpreting the world" that requires a "peculiar intelligence" to the pastoral ministry itself. "The Pastoral Imagination," *Initiatives in Religion* 9 (Spring 2001): 1–2, 15.

37. See http://www.Christianleaders.org.

38. Course information and video samples available at http://www.WesleyMinistryNetwork.com.

Chapter Six: The Play of Pastoral Care

1. For more information about this project, see www.claremontfoundation.org.

2. Alastair Campbell, *Rediscovering Pastoral Care* (Philadelphia: Westminster, 1981), 35. Donald Capps makes the connection between the image of the holy fool and the pastoral practice of reframing. See *A New Method in Pastoral Care* (Minneapolis: Fortress Press, 1990).

3. Campbell, *Rediscovering Pastoral Care*, 55.

4. Ibid., 59.

5. Ibid., 59–62.

6. Jim Dittes, *Re-Calling Ministry*, ed. Donald Capps (St. Louis: Chalice, 1999), 27.

7. Jürgen Moltmann, *Theology of Play* (New York: Harper & Row, 1972), 68.

8. Donald Winnicott, *Playing and Reality* (New York: Basic, 1971), 53.

9. Letty M. Russell, *Church in the Round* (Louisville, Ky.: Westminster/John Knox, 1993), 196.

10. Personal communication with interviewee, 27 August 2001.

11. Thomas Keating, *The Human Condition* (New York: Paulist, 1999), 29.

12. Jerome Berryman, *Godly Play* (San Francisco: Harper & Row, 1991), 257–72.

13. David Augsburger, *Pastoral Counseling across Cultures* (Philadelphia: Westminster, 1986), 17–47.

14. Julia Ching, *Chinese Religions* (Maryknoll, N.Y.: Orbis, 1993), 17.

15. Personal communication with interviewee, 24 July 2001
16. Hugo Rahner, *Man at Play* (London: Burns and Oates, 1965), 11–25.
17. Ibid., 94.   *Humor*
18. Peter Berger, *Redeeming Laughter* (New York: Walter de Gruyter, 1997), 215.
19. Pastoral theologian Donald Capps suggests that humor offers what he calls five psychological "gifts" to religion; humor: saves psychic resources, stimulates identity creation, expresses intimacy, maintains soul, and subtly reframes experience. Donald Capps, *A Time to Laugh: The Religion of Humor* (New York: Continuum, 2005).
20. Berger, *Redeeming Laughter*, 214.
21. Ibid., 200.

Chapter Seven: All I Ever Needed to Know I Learned on the Playground

1. Robert Dykstra has edited a volume that covers a wide variety of metaphors that have guided the practice of pastoral care and counseling for many years. Into this mix, I add my own. This idea is suggested by the material we have covered so far in this book. *Images of Pastoral Care: Classic Readings* (St Louis: Chalice, 2005).
2. Miroslav Volf, *Exclusion and Embrace* (Nashville: Abingdon, 1996), 69.
3. Howard Clinebell, *Ecotherapy* (New York: Haworth, 1996), 34.
4. Ibid., 26.
5. Ibid., 34.
6. Mihaly Csikszentmihalyi, *Creativity* (New York: HarperCollins, 1996), 360–62.
7. Gail R. O'Day, "Commentary of John," in *The New Interpreter's Bible: Luke-John* (Vol. 9) (Nashville; Abingdon Press, 1995), 758.
8. Ibid., 758.
9. Sharon H. Ringe, "Companions in Hope: Spirit and Church in the Fourth Gospel" in *Liberating Eschatology: Essays in Honor of Letty M. Russell*, ed. Margaret A. Farley and Serene Jones (Louisville: Westminster/John Knox, 1999), 181.
10. See Rumi, Jalal al-Din, trans. Coleman Barks with John Moyne, *The Essential Rumi* (New York: HarperCollins, 1995), 36.
11. There are several translations of Brother Lawrence's *Pratique de la présence de Dieu*. I recommend *The Practice of the Presence of God* (Boston: Shambhala, 2005).
12. Julian of Norwich, *Showings,* trans. Edmund Colledge and James Walsh (New York: Paulist, 1978), 225.
13. We often aim to fill this void or emptiness in futile and desperate ways. See Pamela Cooper-White, *Many Voices: Pastoral Psychotherapy in Relational and Theological Perspective* (Minneapolis: Fortress, 2007), 119–24.
14. Several beneficial resources can assist pastoral leaders in the development of care ministries: Leroy Howe, *A Pastor in Every Pew: Equipping Laity for Pastoral Care*

(Valley Forge, Pa.: Judson, 2000); Howard W. Stone, *The Caring Church: A Guide for Lay Pastoral Care* (Minneapolis: Fortress, 1991).

15. Emma Justes suggests that listening is a significant practice of Christian hospitality. See *Hearing beyond the Words* (Nashville: Abingdon, 2006), 1–20.

16. John Cobb, *Beyond Dialogue: Toward a Mutual Transformation of Christianity and Buddhism* (Philadelphia: Fortress Press, 1982), 48.

17. Cobb develops the model in *Beyond Dialogue* through extended research and conversation with Buddhist colleagues.

18. Cobb, *Beyond Dialogue*, 75–118.

19. Ibid., 141.

20. Ibid.

21. Personal conversation at Wesley Seminary, July 2006. See also Marcus Braybrooke, *Christian-Jewish Dialogue: The Next Steps* (London: SCM Press, 2000).

22. Recall phrases such as "turn the other cheek," "repay no one harm," "be angry but do not sin" that appear in the biblical texts. Jesus expressed anger when he overturned the moneychangers' tables in the temple.

23. Carroll Saussy, *The Gift of Anger* (Louisville, Ky.: Westminster John Knox, 1995), 139.

24. Ibid., 141.

25. Ibid., 117.

26. Miroslav Volf, *Exclusion and Embrace: A Theological Exploration of Identity, Otherness, and Reconciliation* (Nashville: Abingdon, 1996).

27. Volf notes levels of exclusion, from not being included because one is not "seen" by the other, to seeing the other and intentionally and willfully excluding so as to inflect harm. Ibid., 67, 72ff.

28. There are two aspects of exclusion according to Volf: (1) Exclusion can "entail cutting of the bonds that connect, taking oneself out of the pattern of interdependence and placing oneself in a position of sovereign independence." This aspect can involve an enemy that needs to be driven away or a nonentity that can be disregarded or abandoned. (2) Exclusion can "entail erasure of separation, not recognizing the other as someone who in his or her otherness belongs to the pattern of interdependence." The other then emerges as an inferior being who must be either assimilated by being made like the self or be subjugated to the self. Volf identifies this as the bare-bones sketch of what exclusion is. Ibid., 67.

29. Ibid.,129.

30. Ibid., 140–47.

Index

anger. *See* emotion

Augsburger, David, 128n13, 134n13

Bible: characters in, 1, 38, 44, 74, 75; studies, 63, 95–96; and pastoral care, 92

boundaries: professional, 16; in play ministry, 49, 62, 64, 81, 83; 106

Campbell, Alastair, 92

Capps, Donald, 134n2, 135n19

Carroll, Jackson, 131n3, 133n24

change, as negative image, vii; institutional, 3–4, 17, 73–75, 78–80, 94, 111; personal, 11, 28, 35, 75, 84, 111, 124;

characters: in dramatic play, 17, 38–44, 47, 52; as psychic reality, 44

child, as symbol, 1–3, 18

Clinebell, Howard, 108–9

Cobb, John B., Jr., 118–19

Cox, Harvey, 130n2

creativity: of persons, 4, 7, 21, 31, 35, 38, 46, 57, 83, 86, 103, 112; of God, 77–78, 81

Csikszentmihalyi, Mihaly, 86

death, 29–30, 41, 84

depleted, vii–viii, 3, 35

depression and ministry, 25–26; 30, 34, 53

discipleship, 88

Dombkowski Hopkins, Denise, 119

dreams: images for ministry, viii; 96; working with, 74–75; and covenant community, 87; God's, 117

Dykstra, Craig, 35, 86

Dykstra, Robert, 135n1

education; adult, 109; practices, 57–60, 62–66, 70, 86–87; theater 46–47; theology, 57, 93

emotion: anger, viii, 24–25, 30, 91, 102, 121–123; grief, 30–31; reclaiming and expressing, 24–29, 63; in dramatic interpretation, 51; intelligence of, 26–27, 72; shame, 31–33

empathy, 27, 42

enjoyment, 6, 14, 22, 37, 40, 47, 59, 68, 101, 107, 123

environment, as context for play, 80–81, 94, 103, 106, 108, 110, 112, 125

Erikson, Erik, 129n18

expectations, vii–viii, 2, 23, 32, 72, 85, 92, 107, 114

fool: holy, 92–93; -ish, 6, 41, 102

Fox, Matthew, 127n4

freedom, 13, 60–61, 66, 76–77, 94, 102, 117, 123

Freud, Sigmund, 61